SUBMARINES, SECRETS & A DARING RESCUE

American Revolutionary War Adventures

SUBMARINES, SECRETS & A DARING RESCUE

Written by Robert J. Skead
with Robert A. Skead

ZONDER**kidz**

ZONDERKIDZ

Submarines, Secrets and a Daring Rescue
Copyright © 2015 by Robert J. Skead
Illustrations © 2015 by Wilson Ong

This title also available as a Zondervan ebook. Visit www.zondervan.com/ebooks.

Requests for information should be addressed to:

Zonderkidz, 3900 Sparks Dr. SE, Grand Rapids, Michigan 49546

ISBN 978-0-310-74747-5

All Scripture quotations, unless otherwise indicated, are from the *King James Version* of the Bible.

Cover design: Deborah Washburn
Cover and interior illustration: Wilson Ong
Interior design and composition: Greg Johnson/Textbook Perfect

Printed in the United States of America

15 16 17 18 19 20 21 22 23 24 /DCI/ 20 19 18 17 16 15 14 13 12 11 10 9 8 7 6 5 4 3 2 1

For my wife, Cherie, who rescued my heart

CONTENTS

CHAPTER 1

THE WATCHING EYES

Glastonbury, Connecticut
April, 1778

Ambrose Clark felt the cold, sharp blade of a bayonet on the back of his neck. "Both of you, be quiet," a voice hissed in his ear. "Don't move a muscle."

Ambrose froze, his heart pounding. His twin brother John had turned and was looking at the man behind Ambrose, his mouth open slightly in shock. Beyond him, in the darkness, Ambrose could make out a small room stacked high with wooden kegs.

"Don't say a word either." The owner of the bayonet grabbed Ambrose's upper arm and shifted the blade to the side of his neck. Not hard enough to slice a layer of skin, but hard enough to send a message that he was quite serious.

Ambrose's mind raced. Was this man friend or foe? He

9

knew John was wondering the exact same thing. *Don't do anything stupid John . . . like attack this guy. I like my neck. And I like my blood inside my body where it belongs.* The blade had been placed directly over Ambrose's jugular vein. With one quick slice, he could be dead.

"Don't even think about doing anything rash to help your comrade here." The man did not speak loudly, but Ambrose did not doubt the seriousness of his threats. "If my blade doesn't kill, it could easily cripple." The man's voice was gruff and deep, belonging to someone older and seasoned in combat.

Ambrose looked at John, who nodded slowly at the man. How did they not hear this man get behind them? The feat seemed impossible to Ambrose. His senses had been on high alert for the past fifteen minutes as they approached the dark buildings of the Stocking gristmill and gunpowder factory. He had only walked ten feet inside the building when he was met by that voice and blade. Had he been hiding in the dark somewhere inside or outside? How did he move so quietly with not even the wooden floor beneath him creaking? More than anything Ambrose wanted to tell the man who they were and why they were there. But he had told them not to speak. His eyes drifted slowly to John who matched his steady look. Through the shadows and over his twin's shoulder he could barely make out the image of large wood and iron machinery. Ambrose took a chance and opened his mouth to speak.

"We—" The blade stung as it pressed harder into his

neck, and he quickly swallowed the rest of his sentence. Ambrose felt beads of sweat run down his forehead and the slope of his nose. His tan cotton shirt dampened with per-spiration. If only their brother Berty were inside with them.

"I said don't make a sound," the man hissed. "Now, when I tell you to move I want you both to walk slowly to the door you just used to get in here. Remember, this is a gunpowder factory. Don't even think about using that pistol you have tucked in your pants, young man," he said to John. "One false move with that and we could all meet our Maker in an instant. Now, move slowly and quietly." A hand waved in Ambrose's peripheral vision, and John started walking. Then Ambrose felt a nudge in his lower back.

Ambrose slowly turned and followed his brother toward the door. Of all the doors to enter this place, they had to choose the one guarded by a watchman with Indian-like skills and a sharp bayonet—who was obviously not afraid to use it first and ask questions later. They had no choice but to follow his commands. If only Ambrose had his knife. Then he could show this guy what a super sharp blade looked like. If there was one skill Ambrose had greater than most it was his ability to strike the smallest target with his knife. The ability had won him bets of skill with men twice his size and age. But it was no good wishing for it now. Ambrose stepped carefully so no sudden movements or tripping would make the blade on his neck accidentally draw blood. The floor under his feet creaked. Why hadn't they heard it when the man snuck across the boards behind them?

Ambrose exited the building behind John and stepped into the dim light of a half moon. He knew his brother felt helpless. The feel of smooth dirt was under his feet as he took a few steps forward. Large rocks trimmed garden beds that looked like they wanted to bloom. Ambrose listened to the sound of Roaring Brook trickling beside them. The large wheel that had operated the gristmill stood still, deactivated during nonworking hours. The water running over the rocks sounded like tiny voices calling to him. If only he could speak too.

Down the road, Berty Clark held the reins of the three horses belonging to him and his two younger brothers. What was taking them so long? All they had to do was find George Stocking, wake him up, and deliver the message from Colonel Sherburne. He hoped they weren't just being shy about waking someone up. *Kids.* You give them the freedom to do something on their own and they screw it up. But Berty decided to be patient a little while longer. Perhaps Stocking was not at home. He'd give them fifteen more minutes. If they weren't back by then, he'd wake everybody up and embarrass the twins at the same time.

"What are you doing on this property?" the voice asked.

"Finally," Ambrose and John said in unison.

"We can talk now?" Ambrose reached up slowly to touch his neck. "In that case, I respectfully ask that you remove the blade you hold so firmly on my neck." He still hadn't seen the face of his captor, and he had to fight the urge to spin around.

"Not yet," said the man. "Explain yourselves first."

"We are courier volunteers for the Connecticut Militia," John said. "We carry a special message from Colonel Sherburne for George Stocking, Senior. It's in my left pants pocket. May I get it for you?"

"No, keep your hands above your heads and proceed to that building straight ahead. Go quietly and slowly." The man nudged Ambrose a little with the blade.

Ambrose's mouth fell open. How could this man ignore such a statement? They were on official Continental Army business. His eyes met John's. Could they be in the hands of a Loyalist? How could such a person be in control of the gunpowder factory? It was late at night. Perhaps they had stumbled upon a thief.

He matched John's slow pace as he walked toward the brown building fifty feet away on the north side of the property. Every few steps he turned and looked back at Ambrose and their captor who trudged behind with his bayonet still firmly placed near Ambrose's neck.

"Knock six times," the voice ordered when they reached the door.

"This was the door I suggested we go to," John whispered to Ambrose. "But no, you had to—"

Ambrose felt the knife push a little harder into his skin. "Shut up, brother."

"Yes, shut up, both of you." The man still had a firm grip on Ambrose's upper arm. "Knock," the man repeated.

John raised his arm and knocked slowly six times.

A few moments passed, then—

"Yes, what is it?" The voice inside sounded annoyed and tired.

"It's Cooper. I have two intruders who claim to have a message for you from Colonel Sherburne, but they entered the main powder building without authority. I don't know how they got past the outside watchmen, but I will attend to them later," Cooper said with an irritated tone.

The door opened revealing a tall, muscular man with silver hair, naturally parted on the side. It looked disheveled, probably from sleep. "Let them in, but keep your weapon at the ready."

Ambrose walked stiffly inside the room behind John, all too aware of the bayonet that still pricked his neck.

"I'm George Stocking, Senior," said the man, placing his lantern upon a table. He nodded to their captor, Cooper, who offered a pleasant smile and released the blade from Ambrose's neck, but he kept it out and ready. Ambrose nodded as his eyes zeroed in on Cooper. The man was tall and wiry with short brown hair. He appeared to be in his early thirties. He looked like he could race a rabbit and win.

Mr. Stocking studied the boys. "Hmmm. It's not often one gets to see identical twins." He leaned in closer. "Alike in every way . . . except for that scar." He gazed at the puckered white scar that ran down John's right cheek.

"And our ability to choose the right door to enter." John glared at Ambrose.

Ambrose placed his hand on his neck and gently massaged it. "Hey, I'm the one who had the knife poking at him, brother." He checked his palm in the dim light for any sign of blood.

John turned to Mr. Stocking. "I have the letter." As he reached into his pants pocket, which was close to the pistol tucked inside his belt, Cooper jumped forward and held his bayonet inches from John's neck. John froze.

Mr. Stocking sighed. "Precautionary measures." He waved for him to continue.

John carefully took the letter out.

Ambrose hoped they could do this fast. He knew Berty would be growing impatient. It didn't take much for the twins to set Berty off. Should they tell their older brother about this? Probably best not to.

"Both of you . . . place your hands on the bench and stand still," said Stocking, as he took the letter from John and slowly unfolded it. He took it closer to the lantern. A small grin appeared on his face, and Ambrose felt a wave of relief. *Now he knows we are who we say we are.*

"You'll have to forgive our tight security," said Mr. Stocking, setting the letter on the bench. "When one is operating a secret gunpowder factory for the Continental Army, one can't be too careful. Our security and safety precautions are extreme but necessary. We can't have Loyalists or the Redcoats finding out we are not an ordinary gristmill." He smiled grimly. "Manufacturing highly explosive powder for Continental Army and militia firearms is our privilege but a dangerous family business. No visitor can get too close."

"If you weren't kids, you'd not still be alive," Cooper said. "Nobody gets to the gristmill."

"Cooper is the best at what he does, which is why we hired him," Mr. Stocking said. "This is dangerous work on many fronts. Any spark could set off a serious explosion, so we must be careful." He studied the twins. "You must be special people if they trusted you with this message."

"Thank you, sir. Yes, the Colonel trusts us and our family." Ambrose's gaze traveled around the small room. Behind Mr. Stocking stood two large bookcases that overflowed with books. Several opened books sat on a desk crowded with papers. "He . . . um . . . told me what was in the letter in case anything happened to my brother here . . . so I could get the message to you as well," Ambrose turned his attention away from the gunpowder maker for an instant and flashed his brown eyes at his brother.

"He did?" John blurted, eyes full of surprise.

"Yeah," Ambrose replied. "Don't be offended. It was the first time he ever did that." Ambrose turned to Mr. Stocking. "It's our father's orders that we always stay together and work as a team." He paused and stood straighter. "The colonel has a dire need to get some powder to his troops, especially those under the command of General Silliman who is expecting a raid by the Redcoats along the Connecticut towns by the Long Island Sound."

Stocking smiled and walked to a table where he secured a sheet of paper, a quill, and ink. He quickly penned a note and turned to the boys. "This is my reply to the Colonel. We have stock ready to move, but I need the Colonel to provide the appropriate escort to safely move it where it's needed. There are many unscrupulous characters who would love to make their fortunes by selling this powder to the Brits or Loyalists. Now . . ." He turned to the security guard. "Cooper, please show the couriers the way out."

Ambrose grinned and followed Cooper's lead. John walked right behind him.

Once outside, Cooper looked around. "Where are your horses?"

"With our brother down the road," John said. "We didn't want to gallop in during the middle of the night and wake everyone up."

"That was wise," Cooper said. "Don't be surprised if you meet up with my watchmen on the way off the property, unless they are like Christ's disciples and have fallen asleep on their watch." His expression grew hard. "Either way, they will be punished for allowing you to get this far." He walked briskly towards the gate.

Ambrose jogged to catch up. "I have to ask you . . ." He hesitated. "You snuck up on us back there . . . how'd you do that?"

Cooper stopped and looked at Ambrose and the corners of his mouth twitched. "I was trained by Indians in the last war," he said, with a sound that resembled a small laugh. "Let's just leave it at that."

"I'd love to be able to do that," Ambrose admitted.

"You must learn to think and move like a cat." Cooper narrowed his eyes and lowered his body.

Ambrose nodded, but he wondered if it was really that simple. Cooper seemed to glide across the courtyard as though his feet never even touched the ground.

"If you had made a false move in there, I would have cut you both and had your scalps hanging on my trophy wall," Cooper stated, matter-of-factly. He pointed with his finger toward the road out. "You're on your own from here." Closing the gate, he headed back toward Mr. Stocking's house.

Ambrose ran his fingers through his hair. "Good for us, we didn't make a false move."

"Good for you too, Mr. Cooper," John said. "Then you'd have had to deal with our mother."

Cooper turned and jerked a nod.

Ambrose could tell Cooper held back a laugh. Obviously the man's tough exterior and intensity didn't stop him from appreciating a good quip. He knew the security man trusted them now and maybe even liked them.

At the gate, the boys nodded goodbye to Cooper and walked down the rocky dirt road.

Ambrose tucked Stocking's response into his pocket.

Soon, he spotted the outlines of their older brother Berty and their horses coming toward them. But what neither he nor his brothers saw was the man hidden in the woods, watching them.

CHAPTER 2

FROM BEHIND THE TREE

He had been following them for a full day, always staying far enough behind so as not to be noticed. He'd done his research on the Clark family. Lamberton, the father, had been "mysteriously" shot and wounded and was still recuperating at home. Not a current threat, his colleagues would follow the elder Lamberton's activities should he stray from home and resume his covert missions for the Continentals.

No, he was more interested in the activities of Lamberton's sons. Two of them, Enoch and Samuel, didn't seem to be of concern—they knew how to sail and shoot a musket, but were not as skilled in such matters as their father and other brothers. They were more interested in farming. But Berty and the twins were different. He'd discovered Berty was a member of the Connecticut militia and the twins, well, their special skills could certainly be a threat to the British. He knew that well.

The man inhaled a breath of cold air. His black steed with white legs quietly nibbled the tall, dew-covered grass. Yes, he'd chip away at the rebel family, one by one—and relish every moment.

First, he'd use his informants and expert training to gather any and all information to help his cause. The fools had just led him to the colonials' secret gunpowder factory. He had heard there were four such mills in Connecticut, and now he had the first one in his sights.

The security detail he'd evaded on the property had made it obvious to him this wasn't an ordinary gristmill. Soon, his associates would make sure it was no more. And it would be so easy to make it look like an accident. First, they'd take what they could for British muskets and canons and then—boom!

He gazed through his telescope at the three Clark boys chatting on the road. One of the younger ones bore a scar on his cheek. He and his brothers would be feeling more pain soon enough.

CHAPTER 3

SHOTS IN THE NIGHT

What took you two idiots so long?" Berty asked, sounding like the typical annoyed older brother. He strode toward them, holding the reins of their three horses.

"Um . . . we felt bad about waking people up," John replied. He grabbed the bridle of his mare, Sweetcake, and took the reins from Berty.

"Knew it," Berty said. "You see, Fifer," Berty often called Ambrose by the nickname he had earned as a result of his expertise at playing the fife. "This is exactly why you need me to babysit you." Berty patted his gray-and-white horse, Goliath. "Let's go find a place to camp and head back to Sherburne's at daylight, then home. You have Stocking's reply, right?"

"Yes," Ambrose replied, tapping his pocket. Ambrose kissed his mare, Muffin, on the snout, and glared at Berty.

"And we can take care of ourselves, Berty." He jerked Muffin's reins from his older brother's hands.

Ambrose knew that Berty trusted them, but he usually pretended as though he didn't. He was twenty-three, after all—eight years older. He liked to keep his younger brothers in line. Still, Ambrose knew Berty would never forget about the special mission Ambrose and John had gone on for their dad, the one where they had gotten to meet General George Washington—and even help save his life. Not even Berty could say he'd done that.

John rubbed his horse's neck and Ambrose grinned. Just like himself with Muffin, John had taken a strong liking to Sweetcake the day he'd gotten her. It was the day after they'd completed their first mission, and the man who'd given them their horses was very special—General George Washington himself.

As they prepared to mount their horses and leave, a shot rang out.

Ambrose stiffened, quickly pulling Muffin closer. She stamped the ground nervously and snorted in his ear. He looked at John, who was gripping the reins of his horse, his eyes wide. Beside him, Berty drew his pistol, motioning for the twins to keep quiet.

Ambrose peered into the darkness to their left. All he could see in the crisp night air were the short puffs of his breath illuminated by moonlight.

John pulled his pistol from his belt and raised it.

Another shot echoed, followed by a third. Very close.

Too close. The shooters were nearby in the woods. But what or who were they shooting at?

"Get down!" said Berty, placing his horse between himself and the gunfire. His eyes never left the trees to their left.

Knowing his horse would never bolt or step on him, Ambrose threw himself onto the ground, John following suit. Ambrose whispered to his brothers, "Three men." One person could not reload a musket that quickly.

"Hunters . . . shooting at deer?" John suggested.

"Could be," Berty steadied his horse, who was moving restlessly, ears pricked toward the brush. "But—"

The sound of cracking branches interrupted whatever Berty had planned to say. An instant later, a rider on a black horse with white forelegs burst from the woods. The boys' horses jerked. Ambrose jumped to his feet and tugged on the reins to control his skittish mare. His heart beat double time.

The rider was about one hundred feet away. He came to a halt and stared at the boys as if daring them to do something. Then he spun his horse around and sped away in the opposite direction.

The brothers stared after him.

"What was that all about?" Ambrose breathed.

Before anyone could answer, two men on foot crashed through the tall brush. They jumped onto the road, spotted the boys, and immediately ran towards them with muskets pointed at their chests.

"Halt!" one of them, a short and stocky man, bellowed. He squinted through the dark at them as he hiked up his brown trousers by the waist with his left hand.

"Easy there, gentlemen," Berty slowly aimed his pistol at the taller man, as did John. "Let's not start a shooting match," Berty said quickly and calmly.

"You'd be wise to lower your weapons." The tall, muscular man steadied his aim. "If you shoot me, my partner will shoot one of you. And unless you get me straight in the heart, I'll shoot another one of you before I die." He motioned to the twins. "There may be a lot of bloodshed for no reason."

Tense, Berty slowly lowered his weapon.

John kept his weapon raised at the same man.

"You too, son. I don't enjoy killing boys. But I will," the tall man stated plainly.

Reluctantly, John lowered his pistol and dropped it on the ground.

The men seemed to relax a bit but kept their muskets raised as they came closer. The tall one switched his focus—and his musket—to Ambrose, whose stomach tightened as he looked down the barrel of the weapon.

"Well, now. What have we here?" he said, looking Ambrose up and down. "A little late to be out for a ride, ain't it?"

John raised his hands.

"That rider was spying and trespassing," declared the tall man. "You with him?"

If they were concerned with trespassers, they must be the security men Cooper had mentioned. Ambrose grinned.

"What's going on here?" Berty held Goliath steady. "Why were you shooting at that man?"

"Do you guys work for Cooper?" Ambrose started to laugh. Cooper was rushing toward them with his weapon at his side.

"You know Cooper?" said the tall man.

Ambrose laughed again. "Yes, and something tells me that's him heading this way. I don't think he's very happy with you. You see, we got to the house and back without you even noticing."

"What's going on here?" Cooper demanded as he jogged up to the men.

The tall man looked at Ambrose, then John, then Berty. "How do we know you're not with that other fella?"

"Because we're not," Ambrose huffed. "Seeing him bolt out of the woods surprised us as much as seeing you." He nodded to Cooper. "Tell them we're ok."

"They're all right, men," Cooper admitted. "Which is more than I can say for you two." Cooper's tone grew angry.

Berty interjected, "Who was that rider you were shooting at?"

"We don't know," the tall one answered. "He was hiding in the woods, trying to evade us. We split up to try and trap him." He turned to Cooper. "That's how these three must have gotten by us. Bad timing, that's all."

Cooper shook his head in disgust. "Bad watchmen.

That's all. Don't think you're getting away with this. That horseman was obviously spying. And you let him get away!"

"Sorry, sir," the tall man said respectfully.

The tall man's musket was still in Ambrose's face, and he was getting tired of looking down it. Hadn't his life been needlessly threatened enough times already tonight? With bravado he wasn't sure he felt, Ambrose firmly pushed the barrel of the tall man's musket away from him. "You always shoot at strangers? We're on your side." Ambrose sized the men up. "That man was not with us."

Berty secured his pistol. "He's right. We traveled alone. Just here to deliver that message."

Following his brother Berty's lead, John bent down and picked up his gun.

The tall man's gaze sharpened and he glanced from Ambrose to John. "Anyone ever tell you, you two look alike?"

"Only everyone who sees us for the first time." Ambrose glanced at his brother. The Clark boys shared the same straight brown hair, the same nose and jawline. They had the same laugh. But Ambrose considered himself the more adventurous of the two. John valued practicality. And safety.

Something rustled in the brush. The guards started to swing their weapons up, but relaxed as another man appeared from the woods. He held a tricorn hat.

"I just missed that fella! It took a few minutes to find this, but I saw it fall off his head back there." The man, whom Ambrose guessed to be in his thirties, laughed. He walked briskly towards them and swung the hat around his finger, which poked through a musket ball-sized hole. "I shot it right off his head. Shooting at someone riding like the wind on horseback ain't easy."

Finally noting the boys, he paused and looked them over, then turned to the short man. "These boys with that rider? Nice job."

"No, we're not!" said John.

"Look here. There's a name . . ." The man held the hat up into the moonlight. "*CREVANS?* It's burned into the hat band."

Ambrose shook his head. "We don't know anyone by that name."

The man holding the hat looked down the empty road and sighed as he kicked the dirt with his toe. "I still can't believe how lucky that guy was."

Ambrose smiled. He had been shot at once—by a horse thief. The musket ball put a nice hole in his shirt and could have killed him. Instead of luck, he knew Providence had protected him.

Ambrose pondered that thought a bit. If the owner of the hat was a traitor, had Providence protected him too? Or were these men just lousy shots? Of course, shooting at a man while riding a horse at night, with a light breeze and in the cold, would never be easy. But perhaps God had created those circumstances.

He sends rain on the good and bad, I guess.

"You boys are free to go," Cooper announced with a wave of his hand.

"Thank you," John said with a grateful look.

Berty nodded to the guards and mounted Goliath. The twins quickly followed suit. Ambrose steered a restless Muffin in a circle around the men.

Berty tugged on Goliath's reins and looked down at the guards. "If you hadn't stopped us, we might have been able to help capture that man."

The tall man cradled his musket in front of his chest. "We'll spread the word. You can do the same. People will be looking for him. Don't you worry."

The man with the hat placed it on his head and just as quickly took it off. "I just can't wear this. But I will keep it. If we ever catch that traitor, I have the evidence." He looked closely at the twins. "Hey, has anyone ever told you—"

"Yes," Ambrose and John said in unison and rolled their eyes.

CHAPTER 4

DESTINY BECKONS

I've been given a special assignment from General Washington." The voice belonged to Major Benjamin Tallmadge.

Ambrose stood in the next room against the wall of the Clark family dining room, John beside him, listening. Ambrose knew the young major reported directly to George Washington, but he was also a friend of the Clark family. Tallmadge was friends with Berty and had been a Yale classmate of Nathan Hale, who'd been hanged by the British as a spy.

"The general needs your assistance," Tallmadge declared.

Ambrose glanced at John. His twin's eyes shone with excitement. Ambrose knew John had the same thought as was in his own mind. *Don't make a move or sound.* If their father caught them eavesdropping, there would be extra cleanup duty in the barn for sure.

A chair creaked and Major Tallmadge continued, "The patriots living adjacent to the Long Island Sound expect foraging raids from the Loyalists and the Brits living on Long Island. After such a rough winter, the enemy is in desperate need of firewood as well as food and supplies."

"Foraging raids?" It was Berty's voice.

Ambrose felt a little spark of envy. If only he were older, maybe he would be in the next room with the major and his father instead of hiding against a wall.

Lamberton's voice grew frustrated. "I'm sick of the Brits stealing and plundering anything and everything they need from patriot families, farms, and businesses."

His father was clearly disgusted by the Redcoats' and Loyalists' behavior. He had joined the cause of liberty soon after the signing of the Declaration of Independence when the Culper Spy network had recruited him for his sailing ability.

A teacup clinked and Tallmadge spoke. "There will be a statewide call for volunteers to assist the militia under General Silliman in preventing the landing and the anticipated pillaging. As you have just said, Lamberton, there is a history of great damage to property, injury, and death to any who interfere with the raiding parties. There is great concern about the dire need for gunpowder for our militia and volunteers. Without it, we will be helpless."

Ambrose looked at John. Stopping the British raids was

important. So was the gunpowder. He knew that full well. If only he could have gotten a better look at the gunpowder factory. It would be interesting to see how gunpowder was made. But like most of their courier missions, the message to Mr. Stocking needed to be delivered immediately, no matter the time of day or night. Had the timing been different, maybe they would have seen the factory during the day. But that was not meant to be. Ambrose could hear the major's footsteps pacing the room. He inched himself away from the door and nudged John back to ensure they wouldn't be seen.

The footsteps stopped.

Tallmadge said, "I've already taken measures to get as much gunpowder as possible to Silliman and his officers who are scattered along the coast from Norwalk to New London. That's about eighty miles. The Stocking family—the parents and their four sons—have been working at their factory all winter, making and storing gunpowder for us. After the horrible winter we had, many of the roads are now unfit for transporting the powder safely. I'm thinking an escort by water would be best. Which is why I'm here. I need an expert sailor."

Lamberton sighed. "I'm sorry . . . my shoulder's still not one hundred percent recovered. I'm not strong enough to grip the tiller or hoist the sails myself."

Ambrose pictured him rotating his arm and testing his shoulder. He knew his father was impatient for it to be healed.

"I'm afraid I can't do it." Their father paused. "Besides, I'm still trying to discover the name of the spy who gave away my last mission."

Ambrose gritted his teeth. *The man who got Dad shot.*

"I was afraid you might say that," Tallmadge said. "If you can't, then who?"

Ambrose's heart skipped a beat. There was only one sailor almost as good as his father.

"The next best sailor in the family is Ambrose, but I'm not going to let *him* do it," Lamberton said. "I've already put my twins in a great deal of danger once. I'm just not sure . . ."

Ambrose's mouth fell open. How could his father not let him go?

"I know about the gunpowder factory," Berty stated confidently.

"You do?" Tallmadge's voice was filled with surprise.

"Yes. As Providence would have it, we met the men who guard the factory a few nights ago. They stopped us while in pursuit of a traitor spy who was snooping around their place. They thought we were the spies."

Tallmadge paced the room. "Interesting." He stopped, close enough that Ambrose could see his shadow fall through the open doorway. Ambrose pressed his back tighter against the wall.

Tallmadge cleared his throat. "Hmm. Maybe Providence is the reason I felt so strongly about having your family involved in this mission. You see, we need an accomplished sailor. Someone we can trust."

"Few men are available, with the war and all," Lamberton said. "Most men are already doing their part."

"James Raimo and Matthew White are fighting in Rhode Island," Berty said.

"Lawrence Petersen is a full-time fisherman. But he wouldn't have the time or inclination . . ." Lamberton's voice drifted in thought. "George Clinton is a suspected Loyalist. He's the only other really qualified sailor in this part of Connecticut. But I don't think . . ."

"No," Tallmadge interjected. "Your son Ambrose . . . his service was exemplary on the courier mission to Washington." He paused. "He is young . . . but brave."

"Brave and rash—"

Rash? Ambrose looked at John who nodded in agreement.

Lamberton's comment was interrupted by Tallmadge. "But apparently trustworthy and available. These are difficult times." Tallmadge paused, letting that thought sink into Lamberton's sharp brain. "General Washington had hoped you might be well enough."

Ambrose's legs twitched excitedly. He was trustworthy and certainly available.

"I'd be doing my country and the mission a disservice if I agreed to go," their father replied. "I wish I were stronger. My answer would certainly have been yes."

"Who else might you recommend then, Lamberton?" Tallmadge asked.

A long pause, then Lamberton sighed. "No one,

unfortunately." He paused again. "There's no one else available as skilled as Ambrose. But he's only fifteen."

"That's right!" Ignoring John's hiss of warning, Ambrose popped out from hiding and stood in the doorway. "No one can sail as well as me."

All eyes turned to him. Ambrose could tell by their stern faces that showing himself might not have been a good idea. And from the smirk on Berty's face, he suspected his older brother had known Ambrose was listening in all along.

Ambrose cleared his throat and straightened. "Because I was trained by the best." He gave his father a half smile. Then he glanced at Major Ben Tallmadge. The major wore a navy blue jacket with yellow trim. His brown hair was worn past his ear lobes and parted down the middle in the fashion of the day.

Berty rolled his eyes. Maybe Ambrose was going to need back-up.

John was still leaning against the wall in the next room. Ignoring his protests, Ambrose grabbed his twin by the shirtsleeve and pulled him out. John heaved a breath and looked apprehensively at their father.

Lamberton stared at the boys. "There will be plenty of horse manure needing your attention in the barn later." He looked directly at Ambrose. "As for the sailing, it's not happening." He turned back to the major. "I put him and his brother in extreme danger once. To do so again . . ." He shook his head.

"I know. I'm hesitant about it as well."

"I've done fine as a courier," Ambrose interjected.

His father made a dismissive gesture. "The recent courier missions I permitted have been routine."

Tallmadge eyed Ambrose thoughtfully. "We do, however, need the best sailor for this excursion. It's out of the ordinary. If you can't do it—"

Berty jumped in. "I'll do it. I can sail."

Ambrose looked at his father, silently pleading. There was no way Berty was as good a sailor as he was, even if Berty *was* eight years older.

Tallmadge was shaking his head at Berty's statement. "I have a few other opportunities in mind for you, my friend." He turned his attention once again back to Lamberton. "I promise you there will be plenty of soldiers around protecting this shipment when it arrives. As with everything we do, this will be a secret only known by a few. I too would never want to risk the safety of your sons. But as you know full well, these are difficult times."

The major and the father were set in a battle of wills for a moment, looking at each other with all seriousness.

Lamberton studied Ambrose a long moment then glanced at John, who stood somewhat uncomfortably at Ambrose's side. At last, he nodded. "All right." Ambrose held his breath. "I'll permit it *only* if John accompanies him. Two are stronger—and less apt to make rash decisions." He looked pointedly at Ambrose. "John tends to be a bit more . . . thoughtful." It was a fact Ambrose knew well.

Standing beside Ambrose, John sighed. Ambrose knew his twin wasn't crazy about the idea of going off on another adventure—no matter how important the mission. But he also knew his brother would do as directed by their father.

"Come on in. Sit down, boys," Lamberton instructed with a sigh. He motioned to the bench where Berty sat.

"You have a knack for trouble, Fifer," Berty whispered when Ambrose approached.

Ambrose smiled and deliberately stepped on Berty's toe as he sat down next to him. He glanced at him. His big brother wasn't only named after their father, Lamberton. He also looked the most like him of all the five Clark boys. Berty and his father had the exact same eyes and hair.

John sat on the other side of their older brother. Ambrose shifted his weight and scratched his brown hair.

Benjamin Tallmadge nodded. "Now that we're all here, I presume you heard me from the beginning?"

"Umm, pretty much, sir," Ambrose fixed his gaze on the major. Tallmadge adjusted the stiff blue coat that covered his white shirt.

"Yes. We're sorry, sir," John assured them.

Ambrose wasn't, but kept quiet.

"Understood. I'll continue. The Stockings have excellent craftsmen who make watertight kegs, each containing twenty-five pounds of powder." Tallmadge started to pace again as he spoke. "The Bushnell brothers—David and Ezra—designed and built a boat that can be submerged under water."

"What?" Ambrose gasped.

"Impossible," Berty murmured.

"It can travel underwater without being seen." Tallmadge grinned. "And it works."

Lamberton nodded. "They called it the *Turtle*."

"It looks like a turtle?" Ambrose asked.

Tallmadge adjusted his coat again and stood in front of the fire. "It resembles a giant turtle, or two extremely large clam shells stuck together."

"*Turtle* does sound better than *Clam*," Ambrose admitted.

Surprisingly, Tallmadge smiled. "But what it looks like doesn't matter. What matters is that it works. It moves underwater undetected." The major looked out the window. "It failed in its first two missions, but that won't happen the next time we use it."

John inched himself away from his brother as if he wanted to distance himself from the situation. "What happened the first times?"

Tallmadge bent down and warmed his hands by the flames in the fireplace. "We attempted to use the vessel to attach a bomb to a British man-of-war in the North River. There were . . . issues getting the bomb attached to the ship." He straightened. "We believe, thanks to the assistance of Ben Franklin, that we have solved that problem."

Tallmadge continued. "We moved the *Turtle* from where it was built in Old Saybrook to the North River. A special wagon with the *Turtle* on board is now heading for Glastonbury."

"So, you'll need an expert sailor who knows the river and the Sound." Ambrose hoped his voice didn't reveal any nervousness. He was up for the challenge but his stomach fluttered with excitement and not a little bit of nerves.

"I need someone to tow the *Turtle*—loaded with kegs of gunpowder—down the Connecticut River from Glastonbury to the Sound and then to a port like Fairfield. From there it can be unloaded and transported by wagon to the various places the troops will be camped and waiting."

Ambrose nodded. "I can do that."

Tallmadge turned to Berty. "I need you, my friend, to lead a land mission as a decoy to divert any would-be thieves, loyalists, or opportunists trying to make a large amount of illicit money by capturing the gunpowder."

Berty straightened up and nodded. "I can do that." He smiled at Ambrose, obviously proud to be part of the mission as well.

"Good. I had a feeling that would be your answer." Tallmadge looked at Lamberton. "The current plan is to have four wagons, each loaded with hay and two kegs of gunpowder hidden beneath. The hay is needed for a small herd of a dozen or so cattle. There would be several mounted militiamen dressed as farmers protecting the convoy. Berty, you'll direct the group. You'll go to the Stockings, pick up the kegs with my men . . . we'll need some kegs with your party, in case anything happens to the *Turtle*. Then you'll lead your diversion team on an overland route to Fairfield."

Berty confidently tugged on the hem of his shirt. "All right."

Tallmadge turned his attention to the twins. "Ambrose

and John, the remainder of the gunpowder—the bulk of it—will be in the *Turtle*, which you will tow with your skiff. It will be hidden that way and not look as suspicious as it would if it were on a barge."

Tallmadge paused thoughtfully then turned to Berty and looked him up and down. "Yes, I believe you will be just the right size and strong enough."

Berty looked at the major quizzically.

Tallmadge grinned. "And even more importantly, you have the strength of character and drive to see this mission through. Berty, one thing I admire about you is you never give up. When your diversion mission is complete, I want you to train with Mr. Bushnell. Learn how to operate the *Turtle*, take it under water . . . and sink a British frigate. *That* will send a message to those Lobsterbacks that we are indeed a threat."

Berty took a breath and glanced away. He allowed himself a small smile. He locked eyes with the major and stuck out his hand. "I can do that too."

The major took hold of Berty's hand and shook it.

Berty looked at his father, the man who inspired his patriotism. "Anything to serve."

"Excellent." Tallmadge clapped his hands once, pleased. "Friends, when you see the *Turtle*, you'll be absolutely amazed."

CHAPTER 5

MEETING THE TURTLE

A brisk wind propelled the Clark family's new 18-foot skiff up the Connecticut River to Glastonbury. The cold, damp feel of the tiller reminded Ambrose it was spring, one of the best times to be on the water, although he'd sail any time of the year. He could steer for hours and never tire. Not even a cold spray of water from the river could wash the grin from his face. Ambrose loved the sleek lines of his family's new craft, which they all pitched in to help build over the past winter. John had done most of the work on it and proved to be an excellent craftsman. The sails had been specially made by one of their father's friends in Boston.

John stood at the bow of the skiff, looking into the water as Ambrose scanned the shoreline through his spyglass. "There it is!"

A pair of black women's britches waved in the wind from a clothesline. Ambrose chuckled. "Women's britches to mark a secret location."

He turned the skiff towards the shore. As he maneuvered the vessel closer, Ambrose spotted a small inlet feeding into the river. Ambrose imagined the *Turtle* gently bobbing above the water's surface somewhere close by, probably attached to a dock by several ropes.

Ambrose sailed down the inlet and dropped the skiff's anchor. Once the boat held firm, he and his brother jumped into the knee-deep water and walked onto the beach. He never used docks if he could avoid it, preferring their vessel rest securely on a beach or in the water and not bouncing against wood. Two guards with muskets appeared on the shore, but when they saw the twins they lowered their weapons, smiled, and waved. Ambrose smiled back. He took in his surroundings. He liked the look of the Stocking gristmill better from this view than from when they first saw it and met Cooper. In front of the tree line stood the small Stocking home, a bunkhouse for workers, several small buildings, storage sheds, and the main mill itself.

When Tallmadge gave him his instructions, he had stated the *Turtle* would be delivered on a special custom-made wagon. Ambrose's heart beat faster. It had to be nearby. Would it actually look like an overgrown clam? Ambrose jogged around the bend thirty feet along the inlet. There it was floating on the water. He stepped onto the dock. He scratched his head as he studied the strange vessel of wood and metal floating in front of them in the water. The top was made of brass. Glass portholes decorated the sides. Two brass tubes pointed toward the sky. It only stuck out about three feet from the water, but Ambrose imagined there was another four or five feet of the watertight vessel beneath the surface.

"It's like nothing I ever imagined," he whispered.

"We're going to tow that?" John asked, jogging up from behind.

"Yes, we are, John boy." Ambrose smiled. "And with kegs of gunpowder as passengers." He clapped his hands together. "Now if that doesn't excite a fellow, I don't know what will."

John was slightly less enthralled. "It's a clam-shaped coffin." He picked up a stone from the beach and threw it into the water. "How do we get ourselves into these situations?"

"Ahoy, there!" a voice called from behind.

Ambrose turned. A scholarly looking man approached. If this was Mr. Bushnell, he wasn't nearly as old as Ambrose had expected. Berty walked along with him. Goliath drank from a trough beside a shed.

"You must be Mr. Bushnell." John extended his hand and the older man shook it.

Ambrose extended his hand. "I'm—"

"You're the Clark twins." Bushnell stopped in front of them and studied Ambrose's face. "I've heard a lot about you. I was pleased to meet your brother here. You must be Ambrose." He turned to John and eyed his scar. "And you are John." He took a step back. "I'm David Bushnell."

Ambrose marveled at the inventor. "We've heard a lot about you too." Ambrose nodded to his brother. "Berty."

Berty grinned. "I just arrived with Goliath thirty minutes ago. Glad you didn't sink our skiff."

"The prince of the high seas actually got us here safely," John said.

Ambrose looked over Berty's shoulder. "Where's Mr. Stocking, Cooper, and the other men we met?"

"Stocking is away on business," Bushnell answered.

"And Cooper was here earlier," Berty added.

Ambrose grinned. He was no doubt somewhere on the property making sure everyone was doing their job and that the grounds were protected.

Bushnell smiled. "Identical twins have always intrigued me. Yes, our Maker is quite an artist." Bushnell rubbed his hands together to warm them. "They call me the Yankee tinkerer, but you can call me Mr. Bushnell. I see you've met our *American Turtle*."

"Only briefly," John admitted.

"How did you get the idea for this thing?" Ambrose walked closer to the *Turtle*.

"The idea for this *thing* came to me at Yale where I studied with and met a number of patriots now actively involved in our cause. Call it a passion, but I became determined to discover ways to destroy enemy ships. In the past, an army could sink a ship with flaming oil or exploding fireballs. I invented a new way . . . by packing gunpowder into a waterproof keg. But I needed a way to deliver it. So more than two years ago, I began secret construction of my *Turtle*. This is my third version of the vessel."

"What happened to the other two?" John looked up.

Bushnell waved his hand. "Don't bother worrying about that, young man. This one is perfect."

"What do you mean 'don't bother'?" John's voice sounded pinched. He glanced at Berty, but Berty didn't seem concerned at all.

Ambrose ignored his brother's anxiety and kept his eyes on the inventor. "Major Tallmadge told us the English have studied the concept of a submarine for centuries."

"Yes, but mine is the first to be used for combat. My *Turtle* is built from weighted planks of wood. And we painted tar into its crevices to make it watertight."

Ambrose gazed at the strange-looking creation and compared it to his skiff.

Bushnell continued, "She's about eight feet across. Six feet high, five feet in middle. We've already loaded her with the gunpowder for your trip."

Ambrose heard the sound of footsteps and turned. Six men walked toward them from a sandy path in the woods. Ambrose quickly glanced at his twin, mouth agape.

"General Washington?" His heart beat like a colonial drum. It was indeed the Commander of the Army. Washington wore his blue dress uniform with brown trousers. He held his tricorn hat firmly onto his head as a gust of wind blew. Behind him marched several soldiers Ambrose recognized as his Life Guards. With them was

Joshua Carpenter. Ambrose's eyes widened with delight at the sight of men he knew.

Pushing aside his surprise, Ambrose threw his shoulders back and stood tall, as did his brothers beside him.

"Good day, everyone." General Washington stuck his hand out and David Bushnell enthusiastically shook it.

"General . . . so good to see you. Quite a surprise," said the scientist.

"Yes, I received word that the Clark boys would be arriving today, so we rode for two days from West Point." General Washington smiled at the twins. "I have a meeting with the governor . . . and I needed to make sure everyone understood the importance of this mission and that gunpowder." He paused and looked deliberately at the Clarks. "If the enemy succeeds in their foraging attacks on Connecticut, it will not only be an act of terrorism but incredibly demoralizing for our cause. The safety of that gunpowder is critical to the citizens of Connecticut and our pursuit of liberty. Do you understand?"

A lump formed in Ambrose's throat. "Yes, sir." He did appreciate the importance—the seriousness—of what they were going to do.

"Yes, I understand too," said John beside him.

"I understand, too, sir," Berty added. "By the way, I'm Berty Clark, their brother. It's a pleasure to meet you, and to lead the diversion team."

Washington nodded. "Nice to meet you. I'm glad you all understand."

Ambrose studied Berty, who stared in awe at General Washington.

Washington adjusted his hat. "We are all fighting for the blessings of liberty for our country and its citizens. The fate of America is at stake. As Mr. Paine wrote, 'Tyranny like hell is not easily conquered. The harder the conflict . . . the more glorious the triumph.'"

Ambrose grinned at John and Berty, knowing his brothers liked the statement as well. They had heard their father quote the same words many times.

Bushnell erupted with enthusiasm, "God save the United States."

Washington broke into a rare grin. "Yes, indeed."

"Our *Turtle* will also bring some hell to the British ships," Bushnell said as he raised a fist enthusiastically.

Washington nodded and strode closer to the *Turtle*. "Yes . . . I agree. Which brings me to my other reason for being here . . . This gives me an opportunity to see my investment up close . . . and wish the boys well." He stopped a few feet from the submarine. "So this is the *American Turtle*." He knelt for a closer look. "Bushnell, you are a man of great mechanical powers." He tilted his head, examining the submarine from every angle. "You have an amazing imagination . . . and are a master craftsman."

"Thank you." Bushnell beamed.

"He has quite an imagination all right," Ambrose said softly to John with a nod. He glanced at the Life Guards who surrounded the general and nodded to Major Gibbs, the man personally responsible for Washington's safety.

"I was disappointed the other missions in the other *Turtle*s didn't prove successful," Washington said. "But I believe escorting the gunpowder in this is a sound idea, and the *Turtle* will someday soon successfully blow up enemy ships and fulfill the vision for which she was crafted."

"Amen to that." Bushnell's eyes brightened.

Ambrose blurted, "I'll amen that. My older brother—"

"Yes, we know." General Washington held up a hand. "That is intelligence we will discuss later." He nodded at Berty.

Washington placed his hand on Bushnell's shoulder. "Does the *Turtle* snap?"

Bushnell grinned. "Never . . . until the word is given."

"And the word is given once she's under that British frigate with a keg of powder beneath her," said a familiar voice. It was Major Gibbs. He took a step toward the twins.

Ambrose smiled at Gibb's dress blue uniform and tan trousers. "I see you're still commanding the general's Life Guards, sir."

"Yes, I am. It's a privilege to do so too." Gibbs nodded at John. "Good to see you again, boys. Nice to make your acquaintance, Mr. Bushnell." Major Gibbs gave a nod to the tinkerer and then to Berty. He stared at the *Turtle* and with conviction added, "Your invention will blow up an enemy ship, strike fear in the hearts of the British, and give us an advantage."

Ambrose took a breath and drank in the major's words. "Well, I believe I can speak for both my brother and myself here in saying we're pleased to be able to help our country by doing our part, sirs."

John nodded. He seemed unable to find words in the presence of General Washington.

"I told you I might call on you again someday," Washington said.

Ambrose remembered the general's words from that day on Van Allen's property in New Jersey just before he and his twin left to return home.

Washington took a deep breath and looked down the inlet. For a brief moment, he closed his eyes and smiled. "In your father's absence, I agree … you were the right patriots for this job." Washington turned to Mr. Bushnell. "I was told earlier my host, the Governor, has a special meal planned for us all, followed by some time for you to rest before you begin your missions. We'll talk more over our meal." Washington waved to the boys. He walked away beside Major Gibbs and leaned in to murmur something in the Major's ear.

Joshua quickly approached the twins. He seemed anxious to talk to them.

"What're you doing here?" Ambrose asked.

"Great to see you again," John exclaimed with a smile.

"Great to see you two as well," Joshua spoke quickly. "So much has happened since I saw you last. I met Major Gibbs and General Washington when they returned the horses you stole. That turned out to be a good thing. We had an interesting conversation . . . then, a few weeks later, I was promoted to Sergeant, transferred to the Dragoons, and now I'll be on the gunpowder diversion mission with your brother."

"That's great," Ambrose and John said in unison.

"It wouldn't have happened if you didn't steal my horse."

Joshua looked over his shoulder. Ambrose saw that the other men, including General Washington, had left the shoreline and were heading toward Stocking's house. "I've got to go," Joshua said, "but I just wanted to tell you that." He waved and jogged after his superiors.

Ambrose struggled for a reply. The rest of that day, Joshua's words replayed in his mind. He stood amazed at how God turned something bad into something good.

▲ ▲ ▲

That evening, General Washington was to spend the night at the home of Governor Jonathan Trumbell at Hartford. The general had arranged for the three Clark brothers to join him and Major Gibbs, David Bushnell and his brother Ezra, and Sergeant Joshua Carpenter for dinner. It was a festive affair. Ambrose sat across the table from the general. The large room was hardly crowded like the Clark family's dining room. If only his father were here to enjoy this company too. Berty raised his eyebrows at Ambrose and glanced at the general's chair. Ambrose grinned. To

Ambrose's delight, they were feasting upon one of his favorite foods—beef and vegetable stew.

After a few minutes of focused eating, Washington took a drink of water and broke the silence. "The weather was so beautiful and welcoming today considering the hard winter we just endured." He looked at Ambrose.

The men around the table all nodded.

"We're all thankful spring is here," Major Gibbs said, reaching for another piece of bread. "Our men need the hope that the change in seasons and weather can bring."

Washington took another drink then said, "Yes, indeed. The rough winter made our army extremely short on supplies…food…clothing…ammunition. Our Continental Congress is working hard to rectify the situation."

"It was a rough winter," Ambrose said. "The worst in fifty years according to our old-timers. I have a good feeling things will get better though."

"Me too." General Washington focused his attention on Ambrose and John. "I'm afraid we must begin our journey tomorrow and return to my men in West Point. Then onto Pennsylvania. I've a feeling we will give chase to the enemy any day. Recent intelligence leads me to think this way." He paused to spoon some stew into his mouth. "Speaking of intelligence, how is your father?"

"He's—" Ambrose and John answered simultaneously. Ambrose stopped in mid-sentence and looked at John. Who should answer? To blurt something at the same time would not show the general the respect he was due.

"He's fine, sir," Berty interjected, leaning around John to look at the general. "He's recuperating at home and should be able to serve again soon."

"He's anxious to resume his duties," Ambrose said.

"He won't sit still very long," John added.

"I know the type," Washington declared. "Please let him know we wish him well."

"I will," all three Clark boys replied simultaneously. The response caused all the men at the table to smile.

"We so appreciate Connecticut's support in the fight for liberty," Washington said to Governor Trumbull. "The food, animals, clothing, and ammunition you and your residents have supplied . . . well, let's just say, while we still need more from every possible source, I shudder to think where we'd be without Connecticut." Washington turned to the Bushnells. "Your state also has great inventive minds committed to the cause."

Governor Trumbull was a round man modestly dressed in a brown jacket and black pants. His face was frank and open, with an ill-trimmed bush of a beard beneath his chin. He paused a moment to make sure the general was finished speaking, then replied, "You have Connecticut's full support, General. We will do whatever it takes to keep those Lobsterbacks from conquering our land and people."

"Yes, the idea of liberty itself is powerful," Washington said. Looking over the dinner guests, he turned his attention to Berty. "I hear you're a key member of your local militia. Any plans to enlist in the Continental Army?"

Berty quickly swallowed his bite of bread. "Yes, sir. I hope to one day be a Dragoon and serve with Major Tallmadge." He paused. "My father hasn't permitted that yet. I didn't know why until I understood his role in the fight for liberty."

"There is a time for everything and I trust your father's wisdom," Washington replied. "You and Sergeant Carpenter will serve together on your secret diversion mission."

Berty and Joshua looked at each other and nodded.

As the dinner conversation wound down, Ambrose casually glanced at General Washington. Would he ever see him again? He hoped with every ounce of his being the answer was yes.

The general politely wiped the corners of his mouth with his napkin. "Thank you, Governor, for your hospitality and for this delicious meal," General Washington said, addressing Mr. Trumbull.

"It was my pleasure," Trumbull replied.

"Well, we all have our jobs to do now." Washington paused and stood. "I must discuss some important matters with the governor alone. You who must stay behind have some training, reviewing, and resting to do."

Major Gibbs began to escort the general toward another room. The twins walked toward the door, until Washington stopped in his tracks and turned to them. "May Providence protect you and guide you on this journey and all you do. We will wait for further intelligence about your towing mission." Washington saluted the twins. "And may I add, as boys becoming young men, keep alive in your hearts that spark of fire called conscience. It will do you well."

With interest in his eyes, Ambrose replied, "We will, sir."

"Yes." John nodded. "Of course."

Washington studied the boys, almost as if he were praying silently. Then, before they could say anything else, he was out of the room. The group he left behind was silent. Ambrose gazed at John and Berty and then David and Ezra Bushnell, and finally Joshua. A burst of breath exploded from Ambrose's lips. It seemed everyone needed a moment to absorb the fact that they had just shared a meal with General George Washington.

CHAPTER 6

GUNPOWDER BRIGADE

The next day at the Stocking homestead, Bushnell schooled the boys on everything that was needed and expected to tow the *Turtle* safely and on the do's and don'ts of dealing with explosives.

Ambrose's stomach fluttered as he heard Bushnell explain how destructive so much gunpowder could be. He and his brother could do this. Hopefully, nothing strange would happen. If it did, he could handle it. There was no one more qualified to accomplish this task than he or his father.

Yes, this would beat any courier mission.

John shook his head at the *Turtle* and Mr. Bushnell.

"It'll be all right, John," Ambrose consoled his brother with a punch to the shoulder. His twin needed to relax and be more like him.

The boys were then ordered to take a nap in Stocking's parlor. They would be operating under cover of night and needed several hours rest so they would be sharp and ready for action. Berty and Joshua spread their blankets on the floor and napped as well.

After their rest, Joshua changed out of his uniform into normal farming clothes of trousers, a tan shirt, and a light jacket. Berty donned a new white cotton shirt, black pants, and jacket. The sun set and the sky turned dark. Berty and Joshua reviewed their plans and route one more time, instructed their escort teams on the mission, and the men carefully loaded their wagons.

Ambrose approached Berty. "Sorry you don't get to babysit us on this trip. Maybe I should be going with you to keep you safe."

"Funny, Fifer. I think we'll be fine," Berty said. He sobered. "Pay attention to everything around you. Be safe. Mother and Father are counting on you two to come back in one piece."

"I'll watch out for him," John grinned.

Ambrose laughed. "I think it's the other way around, brothers."

If he had to, he could do this mission without John's help. Ambrose just knew it. He raised his eyebrows at Berty. "Have fun with your diversion," he said mockingly.

Bushnell laughed. "You boys remind me of me and my brother."

"We have two more brothers at home as well." Ambrose

playfully slapped John's back. "But this is the best-looking one. Well . . . kind of." He threw his arms around Berty. "I love you, big brother."

Berty froze and his arms slowly made their way around Ambrose. Ambrose felt a few hard pats on his back.

"Ah, love you too, Fifer," Berty replied.

Ambrose slowly released his embrace. Aside from John, who for obvious reasons was his closest brother, Berty was his favorite, although he'd never admit it for fear of hurting Enoch or Samuel. Berty, after all, was the one who paid the most attention to him and taught him how to skip rocks and climb trees.

John gave Berty a hug too. "Be well."

"Be well, John," Berty replied with three strong pats on the back.

Ambrose pumped his fist. "Ok . . . let's get our skiff connected to the *Turtle* and get going. I love sailing at night."

This was almost the craziest thing he had ever done, Ambrose decided. He gave a quick glance to the strange-looking vessel trailing twenty feet behind them. More than two hundred and fifty pounds of gunpowder rested within the little *Turtle*. Gunpowder that could explode and kill them if it were ignited. Or be rendered unusable if it got wet.

Still, they had sailed for ten miles, and so far, everything had gone smoothly for the first two-and-a half hours of the voyage. The plan was working. Even in the dark, Ambrose skillfully maneuvered his craft to avoid thin channels, sand bars, and several large boulders. He caught enough wind blowing over the stern to keep them moving steadily and swiftly even with the heavy cargo. Ambrose smiled as the wind streamed through his hair. He was the right man, or boy, for the job. There was no doubt. He felt that there wasn't anything he couldn't do. Someday he'd tell his kids about it all, and his grandkids.

"I'm glad we're pulling and not riding in that thing," John said, looking over his shoulder. "You just better keep steering clear of any rocks or we'll both be dead."

Ambrose waved his worrywart brother off. "Yeah, yeah."

He knew that gunpowder would ignite soon enough in the muskets and canons of patriots aimed at the enemy. If they were successful. He shivered slightly. Across from him, his brother's brown hair fluttered in the wind as he sat in the bow of the boat and peered through a spyglass. Moonlight reflecting off the water gently illuminated the area around them as they glided with the current down the Connecticut River.

The sail caught a gust of fresh spring wind, and the skiff jolted as it pulled the mostly-hidden *Turtle*. Ambrose caught himself and watched John do the same.

"You really should be sitting on top of the *Turtle* with that wooden pole in case we get into trouble with rocks. You could easily push us away . . . keep it from bumping too hard into them," Ambrose said.

"No way," John answered. "Me? Sit on all that gunpowder? I'm not the crazy one, remember."

Ambrose laughed. He wasn't crazy enough to sit on top of the *Turtle* either. But it would have been a good idea, if there wasn't gunpowder on board. He had towed sloops with broken sails before and dragging any vessel in a river full of boulders and sandbars was never easy. But they'd been doing just fine so far. He felt confident.

Ambrose steered the skiff straight down the middle of the river fighting a strong current. His hand tingled from his tight grip on the tiller. As much as he enjoyed sailing at night, he was looking forward to the morning when he could enjoy the warmth of the sun too.

John put his spyglass in his pocket and took hold of his musket.

"Everything all right?" Ambrose called over to his brother.

"Yeah, I thought I saw a ship in the distance. Just being prepared." John looked back at the *Turtle* and shook his head.

"The shape of that thing makes me think about Aunt Bertha!" Ambrose chuckled. Aunt Bertha could eat a boatload of barrels filled with honey cakes. But the *Turtle* had barrels full of gunpowder made in Glastonbury.

Ambrose gazed back at the *Turtle*. She moved slowly, but she was indeed marvelous—even if her cargo was deadly. Tallmadge's plan was brilliant. Later that day, they would arrive in Fairfield. From there, the powder would be loaded onto wagons and continue the journey on land. It could make all the difference in this war.

Ambrose grinned at John. "I bet you hope Sophie doesn't look like Aunt Bertha someday." Ambrose had accepted the fact that Sophie liked John better, but he still liked teasing his brother about the pretty girl who had caught both their eye. "I'm going to win her back! Just wait and see."

"Ha! Keep dreaming!" John waved his hand. His eyes widened. "Ambrose! Boulders! Twenty feet off starboard!" shouted John.

Ambrose's spine prickled. He bit at his lip. Reacting instantly, he pushed hard on the tiller and steered the skiff left. The boat cleared easily, but, what about the cargo trailing behind them? The *Turtle*, filled with its heavy cargo, wouldn't be able to adjust as quickly.

The wind gusted, increasing their speed, and his stomach clenched. *Oh no . . . would there be enough clearance? If not . . .*

With a silent prayer, he watched the rocks, heart racing. The *Turtle* slid nearer, and John gasped.

Nearer . . . nearer . . .

The *Turtle* cleared the boulders by inches. A burst of air exploded from Ambrose's lips. It had been too close. What could he have done differently? Better? He could think of nothing. He turned to John. Thank God he had him as his lookout. Maybe he was wrong. He needed his brother's help. Without it, he'd be dead right now and the patriots would never receive their gunpowder.

"That was close!" exclaimed John, his face pale. He plunked down on a seat on the inside edge of the skiff. "Maybe I should steer and you should be up here."

"I'm here because I'm the better sailor. You know it!" Ambrose pulled on a rope and the sail tightened.

"We all know *you* know it," John replied. Although he joked, Ambrose saw his twin's hand shaking as he reached to swipe the hair off his brow.

Ambrose steered hard a-port. The skiff jolted and John fell back against the side of the hull. "Not funny!" John pointed his finger at Ambrose as he secured his footing.

Ignoring his brother, Ambrose gazed back at the *Turtle*. Rummaging in his rucksack with his free hand, Ambrose pulled out his fife and, clutching the tiller between his knees, brought it to his lips. He launched into a rendition of "A Mighty Fortress." Seven notes flew beautifully out of the flute, then—

"What are you doing?" John admonished angrily. "Someone might hear that."

Ambrose quickly took his flute away from his lips and lowered his gaze. John was right. How could he have been so foolish? He promised himself to be more careful and not get carried away by his impulses. His father never would have done that. Ambrose thought back to how his family enjoyed sitting together while Enoch played guitar, and Ambrose the fife. They all sang while mom worked at the spinet.

He wondered what Mom and Dad were doing right now.

▲ ▲ ▲

For several more hours and miles, Ambrose captained the vessel. His hand grew tired. He had to stay focused on the task at hand. There'd be time later to rest. He needed to stay alert. Even at that thought, after a few more minutes of staring at the water before him and adjusting the sail to meet the demands of the wind, he became distracted. He watched the ripples of water and wondered what kind of fish swam below him.

"Hey, John."

"What?"

"Do you think fish get tired of seafood?"

John shook his head. "You're weird."

"Yes, I know. Thank you." Ambrose chuckled to himself. His question was serious. His mind drifted to the future. What would he do after the delivery? Being a volunteer courier was important but surely he could do more for the cause. But how much would his father permit? And what about mom? She wouldn't like any of it. What if something bad happened to him? It was best to think positive. He had a lot of life to live. Maybe someday he'd be a Dragoon and fight beside Ben Tallmadge. He glanced toward the tree line of the Connecticut shore. Somewhere in these parts is the girl he'd marry. Where is she? What's her name? Certainly she'll be beautiful, inside and out.

At last they passed by Old Saybrook and ventured into the Long Island Sound. Their craft sailed about half a mile from shore. John held his position as lookout and was doing a fantastic job. No threat seemed possible in this peaceful setting. The thought of a threat, however, put a picture of the British Redcoat who shot his father in his mind. He could still see the man, dressed covertly as a farmer, with Ambrose's knife stuck in his hand and wincing in agony. He was thankful he hadn't killed the man. John had been right—it wasn't who he was. He was glad the Brit was in a Continental jail somewhere or perhaps even dead, hanged by the army. Whether dead or alive he hated the man. Hate was a strong word. One his mother disliked. But he'd never felt an emotion so strongly before, until he laid eyes on that Redcoat who admitted what he had done to their father. That man didn't deserve forgiveness.

The Brit had occupied too much of his thoughts. Ambrose perused the early morning sky and marveled at the stars above him. God was surely an artist. He focused on the smooth water.

Guess our adventure is going to be a relatively calm one this time around, thought Ambrose. *Other than almost getting blown up by rocks.*

He'd barely gotten the thought out when a *boom* echoed in the distance. A glow appeared on the horizon over Connecticut.

"John! Look!" Ambrose pointed toward the tree line.

Flickering red illuminated the sky about a mile away above the tree line, as if from flames.

"I hope that had nothing to do with Berty and the convoy!" John said. His face creased with worry.

Ambrose swallowed. "They should have been way beyond that point by now."

He shouldn't even think such a thing. He turned his attention to the sail and wind, then glanced back at the sky.

Probably just a forest fire. A really big one.

CHAPTER 7

DOUBLE CROSSED

Berty whirled around away from the red-hot flames and covered his head and ears with his hands. The wagon behind him had exploded and burned brightly. He had heard the shot that ignited the gunpowder and knew another one could be coming at his wagon any second. His face felt the blast of heat even from thirty feet away. A plume of dark black smoke rose into the sky. He coughed, fighting for a clean gasp of air.

What lasted only a few moments, felt like forever. Some of his men were dead. There was no doubt. Catching a breath, he swallowed and found his voice. "Take cover, everyone!" he called out to the men in his wagon who could hear him and the ones remaining from the other. Then musket shots echoed around him.

Berty clutched his weapon, when suddenly a second

explosion from another wagon closer behind him knocked him off his bench to the ground, his weapon flying through the air. Head throbbing and ears ringing, Berty searched the ground for his musket. It rested ten feet away to his left. He caught his breath. Above, the dark billows of smoke drifted like clouds. The muffled cries from dying men tugged at his heart. How had this happened? He had to help them! If he could only get them to safety.

Berty slowly scrambled to his feet, scooped up his weapon, and ran beside the wagon wheel. A musket ball splintered a tree behind him. He dove behind a large rock on the side of the road for cover. With a burst of energy, he fired back into the woods aiming at the puffs of smoke coming from one of the enemy's muskets.

Shouting, screaming, and gunfire filled the air.

Berty reloaded his weapon. Someone had tipped the Redcoats or Loyalists off about their plans. There was no other way they'd be ambushed right now. Gunpowder was precious. Surely the enemy wouldn't be firing at the remaining wagons and destroying it all. They'd want some for themselves. Heart pounding, he took stock of his surroundings. Where was Joshua? He had been on the last wagon. His mind whirled as he brought the butt of his musket to his shoulder and lined up a loyalist in its sight. He fired and seconds later saw the man jerk backward and fall to the ground. He quickly took another musket ball and powder from his satchel.

Behind him, Berty heard the cries of one of the men on

his team who had been shot. The dying soldier called for his mother. It wasn't the first time Berty had heard a man cry for his mother when dying. Many Continental Army soldiers and militia were young men. It was only natural. But it tore his heart apart.

Berty's blood ran cold. Somebody was interfering with patriot plans and he was anxious to know who. But that didn't matter now. No—now all that mattered was staying alive.

CHAPTER 8

FROM INSIDE THE WOODS

His informant proved to have accurate information once again. Best of all, the patriot scum would never figure out who was revealing their plans. Of that he was certain. That thought, combined with the screams of patriots dying around him and knowing the gunpowder his team of loyalists were about to snatch from the small band of escorts would soon be theirs, caused his thin lips to purse in a ghost of a smile.

He raised his musket and aimed it at the older Clark boy as the rebel fired back at his men. He could pull the trigger and put an end to Berty. But now was not the time. The remaining patriots were well outnumbered. Many of those men left would be killed. They were traitors, after all. But no . . . not this one. Not Berty Clark. His men would take him prisoner if all went according to plan. He would then be tortured for any information and simply because he was a rebel patriot. He hoped Berty's brothers would find out and feel searing pain in their hearts. Their imaginations would think the worst and rightly so.

There was no pain more intense than knowing a loved one was in danger and suffering and that there was nothing one could do about it. Those kinds of thoughts . . . that kind of truth . . . was torturous and more damaging than any physical trauma could ever be. And that was exactly what he wanted the younger Clark boys, as well as everyone else in the Clark family, to feel, especially their father Lamberton. He knew word would travel back to him that his son had been captured. And in Lamberton's position, he'd know the many unpleasant scenarios that could happen to a captured patriot.

The twins were next on his agenda. They would feel physical pain too, then death.

Soon enough. The time was coming.

He patted his black horse on the side of the neck. His steed affectionately nuzzled him back with its nose. The horse had seen enough battles and heard enough musket fire not to be skittish.

CHAPTER 9

THIEVES ON
THE WATER

A gust of wind blew through Ambrose's hair. He breathed deeply and returned his attention to the dark horizon in front of them. He was grateful they had gotten this far safely. Berty would be just fine, he assured himself as they left the glowing shoreline behind. That fire probably had nothing to do with the gunpowder decoy, and Berty was strong and brave. He could take care of himself. Looking out over the choppy, dark water, Ambrose was sure of one thing: there was nowhere else he'd rather be.

He gazed at the open Sound. It held a larger safe zone and no boulders. He exhaled a deep breath to relax. Ambrose sailed for another hour. The position of the sun told him it was about 8 o'clock in the morning.

"Uh-oh! There's a sail!" John held onto the rail of the skiff with one hand and looked behind them through the spyglass. "And it's heading this way!"

Ambrose positioned his sail to fill with wind. Were the men on the approaching boat friend or foe? If they were foe, he would do his best to outrun them, but their little skiff wasn't exactly built for speed. And with the *Turtle* in tow, escape was nearly impossible.

John watched the ship closely for a few minutes. "I think they're gaining on us," he said nervously and grabbed hold of his musket.

"There's no British flag on it!" Ambrose shouted into the wind.

"That doesn't mean anything!" John replied. "I don't have a good feeling about this."

Ambrose steered in a different direction. After a few minutes, it became clear the larger sloop had matched his course. "Yep. They're following us."

Ambrose shook his head. Raiders? Thieves? Pirates? Privateers? They operated everywhere there was water in the world. "What do you think?" Ambrose shouted.

"We have trouble on our hands!" John exclaimed.

"I agree!" He'd defend the *Turtle* and her cargo at any cost. Maybe these sailors were just curious about why they were moving so slowly. "Maybe they're just going the same way and trusting my route!"

John glanced back at the larger boat. "Could be. I don't suppose you can go any faster?"

Ambrose shook his head. His brother already knew the answer to that question of course. He studied the boat's course. If only he didn't have the heavy cargo, he could easily sail away.

There was nothing they could do. The boys watched as the unknown ship slowly gained on them. Before long, it had whooshed up beside them. Three men were on board. Two aimed muskets in their direction, while the other steered their vessel.

"What's your business here?" a man with a long nose called out, gesturing with his gun. "And what is that you're towing?"

"Um . . ." John stammered. "We've been . . . shad fishing . . . and the catch was so good we loaded it into a big barrel our uncle made. That's what that is."

The man eyed the *Turtle* with suspicion. "Looks like that could hold lots of fish."

"We want some!" a short plump man demanded from the tiller.

John shook his head. "I'm afraid that can't happen right now," he called back. "That thing's a bit fragile. Our uncle's not very good at making things. It could bust if your boat or ours collided with it. That's why we're going so slowly."

Ambrose continued to steer the skiff on a steady course. He followed John's verbal lead. "Um . . . if you're heading over to Long Island, be careful. We saw a whale upset a cruiser a while ago. You could be his next victim!"

"We're heading to Fairfield, just a few miles south of here."

"That's our destination too," Ambrose said truthfully. He turned slightly and gave John a pointed look.

John gestured. "Why don't you go ahead of us? Get a

team of men together to help unload the shad when we get there. We can share some with you then." The skiff skipped in a wave and a wash of spray dampened his face.

"We can sell those fish to British soldiers," the short plump man boasted.

Ambrose overheard the comment spoken by the man at the bow of the boat to his captain, which judging by the reaction of the captain, hadn't been for his ears.

"Drop your sail!" the man shouted. "We're taking some of your haul now!"

Ambrose nodded. "Ok! Hold on!" He couldn't do as he was asked and he surely wouldn't make any theft easy. "What does Dad always say brother?"

"Be prepared?" John replied, with a curious look.

"Yes," Ambrose prompted. "So, do so." Ambrose turned away and studied the current and wind. He pulled on a rope and his sail dropped. The boat slowed.

"Ok. We can do it now!" he called back to the other ship. "We don't want any trouble!"

"Are you crazy?" From John's expression, he already assumed Ambrose was.

Ambrose turned to his brother. "Remember what I just said," he whispered.

John slowly eyed his musket leaning against the hull of their skiff.

The captain released his boat's sail and maneuvered his vessel closer to the Clark's skiff.

Ambrose feared a collision could cause a spark. He prayed

silently. Please, God don't let them bump into the *Turtle*. Kaboom was not the last thing he wanted to hear on earth.

Ambrose kept one eye on the men and one on his brother's jacket fluttering in the wind. The men put their weapons down in preparation for pulling alongside the twins' skiff. If Ambrose didn't do something now, there wouldn't be an opportunity later.

"What are you going to do?" John asked softly. "They'll be hauling on the towline to the *Turtle* soon. If they are selling food to the British, they're Loyalists."

Ambrose nodded grimly. Even if there were simply shad in their cargo, he wouldn't want them to have it. And even though he himself had stolen before (because he had to, to carry out a mission), he hated thieves. These men obviously didn't know with whom they were dealing. The twins weren't just a couple of stupid kids sailing for fun.

John's jacket fluttered faster in the wind. It signaled him that now was the time.

"Get ready with that musket, brother," said Ambrose. John tensed.

With a gasp, Ambrose yanked a rope and the sail rose quickly into the air. A gust of wind filled it and the sloop jolted forward, dragging the *Turtle*, which scraped against the other boat.

Please, Lord, don't let it be hard enough to make it blow!

"Now!" he yelled.

As Ambrose frantically tied off the rope, John scooped up his musket and took aim at the hull of the other boat.

Bang! The wooden hull splintered.

Ambrose grabbed an oar and swung it at the two men reaching for the side of their craft even as the wind began to pull it away. With a cry and a splash, they went overboard, bobbing to the surface a second later.

The captain of the other ship was scrambling to his feet as if searching for a weapon. Ambrose swung back around to see John reloading his gun. "Grab the tiller!" Ambrose instructed his twin.

John gently placed his gun down and maneuvered to steer the vessel.

Ambrose jumped on board the other boat. As soon as he found his balance he was met by the steely eyes of the captain, who raised his musket. Ambrose kicked the weapon out of the man's hands and gave a crashing blow to his stomach, pushing him overboard. Wasting no time, Ambrose grabbed his knife from his side and ran to the sails to make three expert slices, disabling them. He hoped it was the very last time he'd have to cut an enemy's sails.

"Let's get out of here," John shouted as he maneuvered the Clark skiff to the boat's side.

Meanwhile the other men had reached for the back of the boat. Ambrose kicked their hands from the wooden hull and jumped onboard his own craft. He darted to the helm and grabbed the tiller, gently taking control of his skiff.

With a hissing sigh, the wind caused the sail to billow, pulling the skiff forward. Behind them, the *Turtle* dragged against the line, then gently bobbed forward and swung into place behind them.

Ambrose looked back at the other craft. The musket ball had done its job—the men had climbed onto the boat and rushed frantically to plug the hole so it would stop taking on water. Ambrose cupped his hands to his mouth.

"Sorry about the sails, sirs. But these fish are for patriots, not Redcoats!"

"You scum!" The captain raised his musket at Ambrose and took aim.

No shot rang out.

"Wet powder is no man's friend!" John shouted helpfully. "Keep your powder dry!"

Ambrose grinned at him and then looked back. One of the men was swimming toward the *Turtle* as it trailed behind them.

Crack!

Ambrose ducked reflexively as a bullet splashed in front of the swimmer. The man immediately stopped his strokes and doggy paddled back towards his own drifting boat.

Ambrose whirled around. Smoke billowed from his brother's musket.

"Good job, John." His twin gave a weary wave of acknowledgment.

With a deep breath, Ambrose pulled on the rope and tightened the sail. The skiff and the *Turtle* skipped through the waves, leaving the Loyalists behind.

CHAPTER 10

YOU WANT TO
DO WHAT?

The Clark family skiff drifted slowly with the current of the Long Island Sound.

John sat on his stool and looked behind their boat. "I hope that little incident didn't damage the *Turtle*."

"That makes two of us." Ambrose glanced at the position of the sun.

He looked at John. "They're within a good drifting range. They'll be all right."

"Wet. Angry too, for sure." John wiped the mist from his face. "I hope we don't run into them again."

John loved boats almost as much as Ambrose did, and ruining someone's property was tearing him up inside. Ambrose jerked a nod. "You had to do it. Remember what General Washington said when we first met him last summer. 'Sometimes in war we have to do things we never thought possible.'"

"I know." John hugged himself to get warmer. "Let's just get this powder delivered so we can go home."

"The whole thing is so confusing," Ambrose said. "We see those loyal to King George as traitors, and they see us as traitors." He shook his head.

Traitors to what? A mad king in a distant land who cared nothing about his subjects? Why should anyone be loyal to a country he had never seen? America was his home, and he would defend it to the end.

They sailed for several more hours and soon the sun was making its way down to the skyline. John shouted, "There's the marker!" He held the spyglass to his eye while he gripped the rail of the skiff. "We're here!"

Two lanterns swayed gently in the distance—the signal that it was safe to land. Ambrose steered starboard and headed for the shore.

As they approached, he and his twin exchanged a glance. John's hand went to his musket. Major Tallmadge had engineered every step of this mission and designated who would know and be involved. But that didn't mean mistakes couldn't happen and identities be compromised. One couldn't just tell by appearances who was on which side, as they had seen with the fishermen.

A large platform with beams and pulleys stood next to

a brand new dock that must have been built just for this mission. That must be how they planned to hoist the *Turtle*.

The sound of a whippoorwill rang from the woods. Ambrose smiled. That was the expected call. He cupped his hand to his mouth and trilled a reply. They sailed closer as a covered wagon and some men emerged from the woods.

John grabbed his musket and carefully maneuvered down the deck of the skiff. He brushed past Ambrose. "You stink," he said with a sniff.

"And you're not funny," Ambrose said, playfully.

Ambrose caught a glimpse of the raised scar on John's left cheek. Once again, he wished John had never had that run-in with the British soldier who cut his face. If only he had gotten there sooner, maybe that would never have happened. The scar was disfiguring but John didn't care. He respected that about his brother. "You know what *stinks* about being a twin?"

"What?"

"I can never call you ugly."

John made a face, then sat at the rear of the boat and grabbed hold of the rope. He readied himself to untie the *Turtle*.

Ambrose steered the vessel right in front of the lanterns and the dock. The hard part would be timing the drift so the *Turtle* would slide near the dock where several men were already in position to grab the towline.

Ambrose aimed for the shore. John untied the rope from the vessel and threw it to the men on the dock. It fell a few feet to the right, and they missed the catch but scrambled to pick it up and secured the *Turtle*. Ambrose glided his skiff toward the sandy shore where a short, rocky beach turned into grass. Tallmadge had picked the perfect spot. He dropped the sail, and John jumped into the water, reaching back in to pull out the anchor and toss it. The skiff drifted in the wind, but it steadied as the anchor took hold.

As Ambrose tied the sail to the mast, the men positioned the *Turtle* between the beams. Wasting no time, they threaded ropes into pulley systems and, in a matter of moments, the *Turtle* was secured and practically motionless. It was obvious they had done this before. *But not with gunpowder aboard*, Ambrose reminded himself. The carefulness of the men's actions combined with their nervous expressions told Ambrose they knew the dangers involved with so much gunpowder.

Ambrose leapt off the boat, soaking his pants and shirt up to his chest. He shivered in the cold water.

John had already slogged ahead. "I request the assistance of Prince Ambrose, captain extraordinaire," he called. "It'll be dark soon."

"Coming." Ambrose splashed toward his brother, watching the men as he went. Wooden planks formed a ramp that led to the covered wagon. They had the *Turtle* open and were carefully hauling the barrels out of it and carrying them down the ramp.

Intent on the goings-on, Ambrose wasn't watching

where he stepped. He slipped on a wet rock and flailed his arms to steady himself.

"Not used to land, huh?" John raised his eyebrows and put one hand on his hip.

"You're not funny," replied Ambrose. "How many times do I have to remind you?"

Ambrose stepped on the sandy shore and walked closer to the *Turtle*. There was a small gash in the side from where the other sloop had scraped it, but she was still seaworthy. "I hope Mr. Bushnell isn't furious we damaged his invention," he said, turning to John.

"I bet the tinkerer can fix that easily enough," John replied.

"Well done, boys!" a voice called from behind them. They turned to see a man walking their way. He had a long sloping nose, deep-set eyes, and a receding hairline.

Ambrose grinned at the praise. *That must be General Silliman. Gold Silliman. What a great name.*

Ambrose walked up to Silliman, his wet shoes heavy and squishing. "Thank you, sir."

"I trust your voyage was pleasant." Silliman adjusted his brown coat. "We're happy you arrived safe and sound."

"Thanks." John approached his brother. "It wasn't exactly pleasant. But the gunpowder is here unharmed and that's all that matters." He took off his jacket and wrung out the bottom of it in the sand.

Silliman walked closer to the dock. Ambrose and John followed. "Just in time too. A flotilla of British ships was reported moving in the Long Island Sound. Where they are headed is anyone's guess." He paused and looked at the twins. "But our hunch is Fairfield. Most of the men there are in the militia and gone fighting other battles." He gestured to the men handling the kegs. "I'm commanding a nervous bunch of farmers, innkeepers, and merchants. That powder will help protect the coast and, in our cannons and muskets, it will bloody some Lobsterback looters."

A chill ran down Ambrose's spine as a breeze connected with his wet clothes.

The sound of hoof beats approaching had everyone turning. A rider appeared and every man, except the boys and the general, drew a weapon and aimed it at him.

"I'm a patriot rider!" The militiaman pulled on the reins of his horse and jumped off. "General!"

"What is it?" Silliman stepped forward.

The rider reported urgently, "The decoy wagon train made slow progress . . . They were intercepted by a party of loyalists who had rowed a whale boat across the sound. There was a fight and shots hit the kegs of gunpowder." The rider looked down and shook his head respectfully. "The explosions killed several people."

Ambrose looked at John in horror. *Berty.* Could that have been the light they saw earlier?

"The impact of one explosion knocked the leader off his wagon . . . We think he was unconscious."

"Berty?" Ambrose blurted.

"His name was Sergeant Clark." The rider looked from

the boys back to Silliman. "The Loyalists took him and two other soldiers as hostages."

Ambrose's stomach clenched. "That's our brother!" His heart beat rapidly. Hostages didn't last long with the Redcoats. They were hanged, tortured if they were thought to have information, or sent to prison ships where they'd eventually get sick and die. He turned to John, who wore the same look of dismay. And what about Joshua? Could he have been among the dead or captured?

The rider breathed deeply. "We think they're headed back to Long Island." He shook his head. "They got the gunpowder on the other two wagons, General. Four kegs."

"And our remaining men?" the general asked.

"Some of them escaped and forged on to Fairfield. Captain Brown ordered me to leave at once and bring this information to you."

Ambrose opened his mouth to speak, but for once couldn't find the words.

John voiced what he was thinking. "Oh, my g . . ." his voice ran off and shook. "They could hang them all."

Ambrose's heart twisted. What were they going to do? A thousand thoughts raced through his head, but he couldn't seem to grab hold of any of them. Except . . .

They will torture and kill Berty. His eyes welled up with tears. He rubbed his sleeve across his face. He could never tell their mother. His father understood the risks involved when fighting for freedom, but his mother . . .

"Thank you for expediting that message to me, Corporal.

Go take a moment for yourself." Silliman waved to one of his men and gestured toward the rider. "Fetch him some water."

"What are we going to do?" Ambrose asked.

Silliman rubbed his temples. "I'm not sure," he sighed. "I'll send word of this by courier to Major Tallmadge. He has the resources to discover more, and then plans can be made. Our first call of duty is to get this gunpowder you just delivered to those who need it." He straightened up and looked at John and Ambrose in turn. "And if I know Tallmadge, he'll work up a plan to find and recapture the gunpowder taken from us. And those men."

Ambrose sighed. "But Berty's our brother." If only he could have been there to help. Maybe his brother would be all right. Maybe Ambrose could have protected him. Maybe . . .

Beyond Silliman, the men had almost finished loading the last few kegs of powder.

Silliman placed his hand on Ambrose's shoulder. "I know Berty personally. In the battle of Brooklyn, he was a brave soldier. And during our retreat, he held fast while others turned their backs and ran from the Redcoats. Berty is a valuable soul like the other men who are also somebody's brother. All our patriots are somebody's son."

"Yes, sir," Ambrose said, but that didn't make the pain in his gut any less. John squeezed his brother's arm. "Tallmadge will have a plan. He'll know what to do. We have to trust the Lord of all Providence to watch over and protect Berty."

Ambrose's fear suddenly transformed into anger. He gritted his teeth. *That gunpowder I just delivered had better kill some Redcoats.*

His pulse raced double time as he slowly turned and gazed at the *Turtle*. Without her heavy load, she bobbed higher in the water, even with the pulleys holding her tight to the dock.

Maybe . . .

He turned to General Silliman. "Can you do me a favor, sir, and get a message to Mr. Bushnell?"

"Yes, of course," Silliman responded. "What is it that you want?"

"Berty was supposed to be trained by Bushnell to use the *Turtle* for a special mission. Tell Bushnell I want to take his place."

John's head swiveled toward his brother. "You want to do what?"

CHAPTER II

YOU LOOK LIKE JONAH

Ambrose took a step closer to his brother and repeated, "I'm taking Berty's place."

"You're a danger seeker!" John dragged Ambrose by the arm away from the other men. "Are you out of your mind?" he hissed.

Silliman eyed the twins. "I'll let you two discuss the matter." He and the other men walked away toward the *Turtle* and prepared the wagons.

"Get away from me." Ambrose pushed John's hand off him.

John pointed his finger at Ambrose. "You're being reckless."

"Calm down. I am not." He was sick and tired of being called reckless. This wasn't about that. He could do this. He could be like Berty. He'd do it for him. He'd do anything for him, for family, and for liberty. And he'd punish and kill the enemy . . . if the *Turtle* worked.

John's face contorted. "Don't give me that. You are too. You want to ride in that thing and blow up a ship?"

Ambrose paused and considered his plan. "Yes. Yes I do."

"Berty was supposed to do it. Not you. He is older and stronger!" He gestured to the *Turtle*. "You can't operate that thing."

Ambrose crossed his arms. "If it goes in the water, I can sail it."

"That thing goes *under* the water—if it works at all." He ran his hand through his hair. "And you don't know if you can do it."

"I know I'm going to try." Ambrose turned to walk away. John spun him back around.

"Don't touch me!" Ambrose whipped away his brother's grasp.

John stepped in front of Ambrose. "The other two missions failed. They were awfully secret about the details and what happened to those who sat in that thing."

Ambrose shook his head. "That's because they were secret missions. They don't give details about secret missions even after the fact. You know that." Ambrose caught movement out of the corner of his eye. It was Silliman, waving the two of them over.

"Then you're crazy or stupid . . . or both."

"I'm not stupid."

His twin was the stupid one for not understanding.

"Don't be motivated by revenge, Ambrose. We're told to forgive, remember. What is it? 70 x 7 times. That means continually."

"Forgive our enemies?" Ambrose waved his hand at his twin. He headed for the wagons.

"Yes," John replied, his tone firm. "What does your conscience say?" John's words carried over Ambrose's shoulder. For only a second, Ambrose stopped. But as he stood there, General Silliman saluted his messenger and looked inquiringly at Ambrose. Taking a deep breath, Ambrose walked briskly toward him.

"Have you two finished discussing?" the general asked. "We need to head out."

"I'm going to do this," Ambrose announced.

General Silliman nodded. "I'll get word to Bushnell via one of my couriers." He spun quickly on his heel and walked away.

CHAPTER 12

NOTHING BUT DARKNESS

"Where is the rest of the gunpowder?"

Searing pain pulsed through Berty's body as his captor's fist collided with his face again.

Darkness surrounded him. An itchy burlap bag hung over his head. Air exploded from his lungs as another surprise punch collided with his stomach. Blood drained from his arms, which were tied to a rafter high above his head. His wrists were raw. He couldn't feel his hands.

"Where is it?" The demand was punctuated by more blows to Berty's torso. If only he could curl up to protect himself. But each thrust of pain was unexpected, and his body was too stretched. He clenched every muscle in his body. The fact that they were asking told him they didn't know about the *Turtle* and his brothers towing the gunpowder. Which meant their source of information was good—but not complete. That small thought gave him some solace.

Another blow to his stomach came fast and hard. Berty grunted louder, hoping his captors would show some mercy. None came.

Another kick to the stomach.

Berty groaned. Tears streamed down his face from the pain, but he didn't say a word, thankful the burlap sack was pulled over his head. How much pain could he endure? That answer he did not know.

More vicious blows came next, to his side and head. Warm blood dripped from his mouth. He hated the taste of his own blood. He had had several bloody lips from fights in his youth. None compared to what he was feeling now.

"Where is the powder, rebel?"

A kick to his side sent a wave of shock through his body.

Nothing they could do to him would make him say anything that would put his brothers, or that gunpowder, in danger. But had his brothers been successful in their mission? Would he live to know? He wouldn't be piloting the *Turtle* now, that was for sure. Who, besides him, could they count on next?

Another blow connected with Berty's skull, and everything turned black.

CHAPTER 13

ILLUMINATING FUNGUS

Major Tallmadge had arranged for the twins and the *Turtle* to be escorted to the residence of David Bushnell in Old Saybrook, Connecticut, for Ambrose's training. The *Turtle*, of course, traveled only at night via armed militiamen driving its special wagon. The boys traveled alongside on horseback. Ambrose didn't say much to John during the entire two-day trip. Every time John tried to talk him out of it, Ambrose raised his hand and told him to shut his mouth. Ambrose hated being angry with his brother and that John was so frustrated with him. It was the longest either had been with each other and not somehow made the other one laugh or forget about why they were mad at each other. But Ambrose knew in his heart he was right. If his brother thought he sought vengeance and was stupid, so be it.

▲ ▲ ▲

The inside of Bushnell's woodshop twinkled with candle-light. Ambrose scratched his chin. What had he gotten himself into? So many buckets of water littered the floor that Ambrose had to be careful where he stepped unless he wanted another soaked shoe. But the water was a necessary precaution. Everything inside the workshop was flammable, no doubt—and top secret. No windows meant no one could look in. Tools to work with wood, iron, brass, and copper sat on workbenches. The original *Turtle* stood on a platform before him.

"I'm sorry to have learned about your brother. You are quite a brave young man." David Bushnell coughed as he patted Ambrose on the back. He nodded to Major Tallmadge.

"Crazy or stupid is more like it," John murmured from the corner where he sulked.

Ambrose shot a look at his brother, who stared accusingly back at him.

Major Tallmadge placed his hand on the *Turtle*'s side. "Bravery is not about lacking fear. Bravery is about facing fear admirably. But the motivation for one's efforts must be pure in order for God to honor it."

Ambrose caught the major searching his eyes. He looked away.

Tallmadge continued, "However, though we face obstacles and hardships all the time in our quest for independence, I believe our cause is a righteous one, and in the end, we will be victorious."

"I agree wholeheartedly. Now . . ." Mr. Bushnell opened a large door on the side of the *Turtle*. "Let's get started. We adapted this, my original *Turtle*, for training since she's no longer seaworthy."

John walked up to the major, interrupting the lesson. "When do you expect to hear news about our brother?" He crossed his arms.

The major looked at Mr. Bushnell. "News could come at any time. Washington's spies are always at work gathering intelligence." He glanced at John. "I hope to hear something soon."

Ambrose pushed aside his strong emotions about Berty's capture. If anything, he'd try to use them to focus on fulfilling what Berty had agreed to do. He peeked inside the *Turtle* at the confusion of rods, valves, vents, latches, screws, pumps, and pedals. "So how do you operate this thing?"

"The tiller controls the rudder," Bushnell pointed at the wooden lever, "just like in your sailing ships. The foot pedal is like that of a spinning wheel. It's quite simple to operate, actually. The tricky part is estimating the distance to travel under water, and pumping and turning the crank to bring the sub into position under the enemy ship's hull. It can be quite exhausting. One must be strong and able bodied to pilot my *Turtle*."

Ambrose smiled at John, who didn't smile back. "I'm your person, then." He paused. "Will that gash in the other one be okay? It's still watertight, right?"

"Yes, of course. I will fix that with some tar." Bushnell pointed to the side of the vessel. "She's crafted with a tongue and groove construction. Caulked with a material made from rags and fibers soaked in creosote. It's tight as a drum."

Ambrose smiled, feeling assured, as he climbed into the *Turtle* and sat in the cockpit.

"You look like Jonah in the belly of the whale." John frowned.

"Quite right," Bushnell admitted. Tallmadge smiled.

"Let's hope it doesn't spit you out." John strolled over and stuck his head inside. "Jonah found himself in the whale because he was disobedient."

"I am not disobeying anyone." Ambrose gently pushed his brother's head out of the vessel. He was trying not to let his brother's sour attitude get to him, but it wasn't easy.

Bushnell cleared his throat, stopping the brother's bickering, and pointed. "To descend, you place your foot on top of that brass plunger, which releases water pressure. I made that compass and depth gauge myself." He nodded at them.

"You are indeed a craftsman and noble patriot," Tallmadge noted. "I'm glad you're on our side."

Bushnell smiled. "This was an expensive undertaking. As you know, I used much of my own money to create the *Turtle*s. But I'm thankful for General Washington's investment. When Ben Franklin looked at her, he said she was not equaled by anything he had ever heard of or seen." Bushnell glowed with pride.

John's eyes widened. "Coming from Ben Franklin, that's quite a compliment," he said.

"We built the *American Turtle* that is outside to fit two small men," Bushnell said, casually.

Two men? Ambrose thought. *Like two twins?*

Major Tallmadge looked at John. Ambrose watched John stare back at him. But his brother said nothing.

"How long can it stay under water?" Ambrose asked.

Bushnell rubbed his chin. "About forty-five minutes, thanks to an improvement idea from Mr. Franklin. The old *Turtle*s could only stay under for thirty minutes."

Major Tallmadge picked up a copper pipe from the workbench and examined it. "You may need that extra fifteen minutes to accomplish the task," he said, looking up at Ambrose.

"Or to get away," John added.

"Yes," Bushnell agreed. He smiled. "Someday, I believe, men will sail underwater for hours in even bigger ships than the *Turtle*. Maybe even days. But for now . . . forty-five minutes." He pointed to the *Turtle*'s floor. "Under Ambrose's feet, in the *Turtle* he'll be using, will be two hundred pounds of lead . . . ballast or weight that will help the *Turtle* dive under water."

"What about these holes?" Ambrose asked, pointing to the holes near the top of the *Turtle*'s hull.

"Those three holes allow air to enter the *Turtle* when it's moving on the water's surface. Those two brass pipes that extend out of the *Turtle* actually shut themselves off when water gets near the top."

Ambrose fiddled with the tiller. "How do you see in here? When under water, I mean?"

"Exceptional question." Bushnell's grin grew wider. "Natural light through the portholes will, of course, allow you to see when at the surface. But when submerged, the compass and depth finder and the cabin itself will be illuminated by pieces of cork."

"Cork?" John asked. "You have magical cork?" He looked curious in spite of himself.

Bushnell raised his finger. "No. Cork that has met with science. We treat the cork with a fungus that gives off a glowing light of sorts—bioluminescence."

"Fungus." Ambrose chuckled.

Bushnell nodded. His face revealed his pleasure. "That fungus was quite a discovery. It doesn't give off any illumination in winter because of the cold temperature. So the *Turtle* only swims in warmer seasons."

"And the *Turtle* always strikes at night because we have to get it into position by towing it with rowboats." Major Tallmadge walked up to Ambrose. "I'll leave the training of how to operate this craft to its inventor." He paused, and his expression took on a serious tone. "The *HMS Lively*, a British Royal frigate, will be your target. She lies in the New York Harbor now. You will pilot the *Turtle* unseen to the *Lively*, get under her hull, use that device to drill into her side where you will detach a keg of powder and leave it attached to her."

"How does the bomb work?" John asked.

Bushnell stifled an excited laugh. "Inside the keg of gunpowder is a clock, which immediately sets after the *Turtle* is detached from the ship. The detonator will be timed for twenty minutes to give you time to get away."

"You better not be too tired at that point," John said, raising his eyebrows.

Ambrose shook his head. "I won't be. Don't worry."

Bushnell added, "When the clock reaches twenty minutes, a spark mechanism ignites the powder."

"Boom!" Tallmadge threw his hands into the air.

"Good-bye, ship," Bushnell declared. He turned to Ambrose. "You have twenty minutes to get safely away." Bushnell gave a nod. "That's it."

John exhaled deeply. "That's not a lot of time, is it?"

Tallmadge looked from John to Ambrose. "That is one of the reasons the other missions failed. During the first one, the pilot couldn't get the screw to attach to the hull, and during the second one, when the first attempt failed the operator was too exhausted for a second chance."

"That's why you built the next one large enough for two people?" John asked.

"Correct." Bushnell adjusted his black tri-corn hat with white trim. "Or one very strong young adult."

"Like Berty." Tallmadge casually picked up Bushnell's diagrammed sketch of the *Turtle* and studied it in awe.

John took a deep breath and scratched his head.

"I guess I better get it right the first time." Ambrose played with the pump and levers. "I can do this."

"But you won't be doing it alone," John said. "If it can fit both of us, then I'm going with you."

"What?" Ambrose held back a grin. He considered extending his hand and welcoming John aboard, but instead said, "No, John. That's not necessary. I can do this alone."

John placed his hand on the *Turtle*. He turned to the major. "Major Tallmadge, permission to join my brother and take this *Turtle* to blow up His Majesty's royal bottom. The bottom of one of his ships, that is."

Tallmadge and Bushnell smiled. The major saluted. "Permission granted. I can see why General Washington likes you boys."

"Royal bottom." Bushnell chuckled. "I disagree with you, Ambrose. Your brother is funny."

CHAPTER 14

A FATHER'S DREAD

Lamberton Clark stood by his window and watched the cold rain falling in sheets outside. Muddy puddles of water filled every crater and hole on his property. He sat down in his chair, placed his head in his hands, and blinked back the tears welling up in his eyes. Had he gone too far? Had he risked too much and endangered his family to win liberty? A courier had just brought verbal word of his son Berty's capture. Each word struck his heart more painfully than the next. If he only knew where Berty was. If only he hadn't let him go. And his twins . . . his boys who were still young lads were now volunteering for a dangerous mission. Why did they feel returning to the safety of their home would be cowardly? He knew the answer and he didn't like it.

Lamberton wiped the tears from his face with his cold

hand and the sleeve of his shirt. He pulled his Bible off the small circular table that flanked his chair and opened it, hoping some words would speak to him.

"But whoso hearkeneth unto me shall dwell safely, and shall be quiet from fear of evil."

PROVERBS 1:33

Lamberton swallowed the large lump in his throat. His thoughts turned to his wife. She would be back soon from the neighbor's home, when the rain stopped. How could he tell her? Should he tell her? Surely their sons needed her prayers. She had always been so committed to prayer. Their marriage had certainly benefitted from each and every one.

He'd have to find the words to tell her.

God, please help me.

Lamberton drew a long breath and forced himself to his feet. Near the fireplace was a small lead cannonball, about 20 pounds, which Lamberton had been using for exercise. He lifted it over his shoulder in a slow, circular motion. His shoulder had been getting stronger. Should he leave and go help Tallmadge find his son? The major had been anxious for his help for months as a secret courier for the Culper Spy Ring.

What was the right thing to do?

Lamberton prayed for his boys while he tried to piece together the events of the last year. Someone was giving away details, however small or large, about what he and the other spies had been doing. Last year, leaked information had gotten him shot. Did the same person blow the lid off Berty's mission? Would it endanger his other sons?

Who was it? What was he to do? He'd have to discuss it all with Tallmadge again soon.

God, guide me, please. And be with Berty, John, and Ambrose. They need you.

CHAPTER 15

A SNAPPING TURTLE

John and Ambrose trained in the *AmericanTurtleIII* for one full day. The cramped space, hot and stale air, and detailed operational procedures that needed to be memorized all made Ambrose think twice about his decision to volunteer for this mission. But he didn't quit. Berty wouldn't have, and neither would he.

He wouldn't let himself think of what Berty might be going through.

Bushnell and Tallmadge went over every detail of every minute of the mission with the boys.

"When it's over, and presuming we're successful—and alive—how do we get the *Turtle* safely back to shore?" Ambrose asked Bushnell. The four of them stood on Bushnell's dock watching the sun set as the small vessel bobbed in the river beside them.

Tallmadge took off his tri-corn hat and held it in front of him. "Whaleboats. The same way you will arrive."

Bushnell grimaced and looked at the boys. "The second mission had Redcoats chasing after the *Turtle*," he admitted.

"It did?" Ambrose looked at John and then back at the floating *Turtle*. "Then there has to be a faster way to escape than cranking the propeller. We'll be too tired."

Bushnell shook his head. "I'm afraid it's the only option."

"Hmm . . ." Everyone turned as John walked over to a coiled pile of rope on the dock. He crouched down and looked at it. Then his eyebrows rose and he stuck his finger into the air.

"I have an idea that just might work!"

Thanks to a sudden rainstorm, it took much longer than expected to travel to New York by wagon and get into position to launch the vessel into the North River. On the isolated shore, David Bushnell and the ten men who escorted the *Turtle* in the wagon prepared a hearty meal over a fire for the boys. They ate eggs, chicken, biscuits with gravy, and drank plenty of water. They would need their strength.

At three o' clock in the morning, with a slack water tide, Ambrose walked down the short wooden dock and finally slid carefully into the *Turtle*. John followed. Once they were settled, two groups of five men each climbed into two whaleboats and rowed down the river, towing the *Turtle*.

After about an hour, they arrived at a safe distance from the *HMS Lively*—far enough that the whaleboats could not be seen in the darkness. Ambrose peeked out of the *Turtle*'s conning tower. He waved to the men aboard the whaleboats, and they cut the *Turtle* loose. Soon those men would set a buoy and head back to shore. There they would wait with the specially-made wagon that had carried the *Turtle* to the North River.

Ambrose whispered below to John, "Remember: on the return trip, make for the buoy. Don't drift past it, whatever you do."

"I know," John's voice echoed from below.

Ambrose looked up at the night sky. Barely a star could be seen through the broken clouds. He set his sights on the water—distinguished from the dark sky only by an occasional glint of moonlight reflected in the waves. Occasionally, water splashed up the *Turtle*'s side and trickled down the uncovered conning tower.

Once more Ambrose thought about Berty. If only they had news of him. How long did he have before he was hanged or placed on a prisoner-of-war ship? For a moment, Ambrose allowed himself to think the one thing he'd avoided all day: maybe Berty was dead already. Tears welled instantly in his eyes, and he pushed the thought away. Now was not the time for pessimism. Now was the time to be brave.

But the Redcoats were ruthless in how they treated patriot prisoners. Wherever he was, Berty was certainly in pain.

Ambrose ducked inside the *Turtle*. He would be inflicting pain on the Redcoats and their precious warship soon enough. Taking a deep breath, he lowered himself onto a wooden chair built into the cockpit. John sat behind him on a small piece of wood connected to the side of the *Turtle*'s hull. His brother nodded solemnly. "Let's do this." A small wave of water splashed inside and wet Ambrose's hair. John stood up and closed the door.

Ambrose wiped his palm on his shirt. He pumped his foot and began turning the crank of the propeller. Soon his shirt and britches dampened with sweat. He cranked faster for greater speed. With the *Turtle*'s brass tower sticking seven inches out of the water, they were detectable, although the cover of night—or early morning—would help.

John examined the inner walls of the *Turtle*. "The seals and joints seem to be fine. No leaking. That's good." He paused. "Let's hope that's true when we're twenty feet under."

Minutes later, thanks to torchlights on board, the British ship came into sight. The *HMS Lively*. Her twenty guns struck fear in the hearts of men aboard enemy ships and on shorelines. Ambrose's heart raced as he peered out one of the tiny glass windows in the brass tower. A hit from a single cannonball would sink them in an instant. He breathed heavily as the *Turtle* cruised the water's surface.

He believed in the Yankee tinkerer's invention. "Soon the *HMS Lively* won't be so lively," he declared as he continued to crank the propeller.

John leaned over Ambrose's shoulder and looked at the compass. "The British pick rotten names for their ships. We heading the right way?"

"Yes."

"You doing all right?"

"I'm fine." Ambrose adjusted the tiller. Before long, the *HMS Lively* lay only about eighty yards away. The boys could hear voices carrying over the water from the frigate. A film of fog had formed on the porthole windows, probably from all the heat Ambrose was creating cranking the propeller and pumping the pedal. He had to admit he was getting a little tired. Another splash of water sprayed inside. Ambrose left the controls and stuck his head up briefly. He felt instantly cooler.

Ambrose could just make out the flag of the British ship fluttering in the darkness. The smell of salty air filled his nostrils. It had always been one of his favorite smells. That and his mother's apple pie. But tonight it brought him little comfort.

A sailor on watch stood near one of several lanterns on the *Lively*'s deck. Ambrose ducked back down, sat in the cockpit chair, and cranked the propeller right for more speed. He needed to get closer before he closed the hatch and submerged. Once under, then the hard part came— attaching the bomb, arming it . . . and getting safely away.

Ambrose cranked and cranked, stopping on occasion to wipe the sweat from his forehead.

"There it is!" a voice shouted from above.

Ambrose stopped cranking and looked at John. "Huh? He didn't say 'What is it?' If you saw this strange-looking thing, you'd say 'What's that?' wouldn't you?"

John looked just as startled as he was. For one second, they stared at each other. Then John jumped up, climbed the small ladder, and closed the round hatch door. "That only means one thing," he said as he quickly locked the hinge and bolted the inside screws. He threw himself down on his small platform and braced himself. "They knew we were coming."

But how?

Heart racing, Ambrose pumped his floor pedal hard. Water filled the bottom tank of the *Turtle*, and the craft dove beneath the waves.

The muffled sound of gunfire rattled above. Musket balls plunked into the water around them.

"You're not retreating?" John asked from behind him.

Ambrose's eyes narrowed. "No. We're going down."

John took a deep breath but said nothing. Ambrose could only hope his brother wouldn't hate him for this later.

How do they keep getting information about what we're doing? thought Ambrose as he watched the surface of the water disappear above them. Who was leaking the details of their plans? But there was no time to worry about that now. He would show them—all of them. *This is for you, Berty.*

The special cork inside the craft illuminated like fire-flies, giving just enough light to see. He pushed again on the pedal. More seawater flooded the bottom tank of the *Turtle* and they sank deeper. Ambrose didn't quite under-stand how everything worked but was glad it did. "We can't talk much . . . submerged . . . to save oxygen."

Stay on course. Move the tiller. Keep the propeller turning. Ambrose struggled to remain on course as he fought strong tides. He focused on his target through the porthole in front of him. "We have a little less than forty-five minutes of air."

John placed his hand on Ambrose's shoulder and squeezed.

"There she is." Ambrose steered his vessel straight toward the bottom of the ship. They were almost fifteen feet below the surface of the water, breathing, and alive. Ambrose turned around and smiled at his brother. He looked around the inside of the craft. "The corks are glow-ing brighter."

John leaned forward to examine one. "Remarkable."

Moments later, the *Turtle* bumped softly against the hull of the warship. The brothers looked at each other.

"Even if they heard that there's nothing they can do." Ambrose pushed the pedal again. The *Turtle* sank deeper and gently brushed against the bottom of the ship. He checked the depth gauge, softly illuminated by fungus. "We're twenty feet below now."

He felt the giant screw touch and scratch across the hull of the ship.

This is it.

Ambrose motioned for John to work the detachable auger, the device that would screw into the ship's hull. As Ambrose cranked the propeller steadily against the current and held the sub in place, John winced as he turned the augur rapidly with all his might and twisted the screw into the ship. "I've done it," he finally acknowledged.

"Great. Just think: outside the hull, that screw is connected to a keg of a hundred and fifty pounds of gunpowder." Ambrose grinned. "Bushnell set the detonation time to twenty minutes."

The air inside the *Turtle* was hot and stale. Sweat ran down Ambrose's back beneath his already saturated shirt, and his clammy britches clung to his legs. His muscles strained as he cranked. He looked at John and nodded. "Okay. Untwist and detach the mine."

John grabbed hold of the rope. "Let's hope this doesn't become our underwater coffin." He pulled the rope hard . . . and the *Turtle* detached from the ship.

Ambrose imagined the clock inside the keg of waterproofed gunpowder beginning to tick down. He didn't want to be anywhere close by when that thing went off. "Let's get out of here!"

John stepped toward the cockpit chair. "Time to trade spots."

Exhausted, Ambrose left the chair and dropped onto the other platform as John took the helm and cranked the propeller, maneuvering the *Turtle* away from the British frigate.

Before long, beads of sweat dripped from John's face and soaked the front of his shirt. "This current is tough to fight."

"You're telling me." Ambrose leaned against the side of the craft and closed his eyes. "No one else got this far. Let's just hope that mine detonates."

John turned and grinned. "Bushnell the tinkerer will be ecstatic."

"Did I just see you smile?" Ambrose asked, cracking open one eye.

"No, not really." John's face strained as he cranked and pumped. "Trust me. This isn't my idea of fun."

"Keep pumping, brother." Ambrose really did feel like Jonah in the belly of the whale. He longed to be spit out, but only as they had planned.

Minutes later, John hit a valve and the *Turtle* popped violently to the surface. Ambrose's stomach lurched. He stood and peered out the porthole. The sun was rising in the east and on the horizon the clouds were streaked with pink. He looked behind them and his heart sank. "We have company."

Several rowboats filled with men in red coats bobbed in the water around the ship. A few now rowed after them, only about one hundred yards away.

"What?" John cranked the propeller furiously.

Ambrose could feel himself sweating anew. "Redcoats in rowboats."

"Release the other mine." John nodded at the cord that was attached to one additional mine on the outside of the *Turtle*.

Ambrose pulled the rope and it released. "It's timed for only four minutes." Ambrose peered out the porthole. "It's drifting in the current behind us, so don't slow down."

"I'm cranking as fast as I can here."

Ambrose peered through the porthole, while John propelled the *Turtle*. Several minutes passed, then—

Kaboom!

The explosion rocked the harbor. Water and debris from two wooden rowboats soared into the air.

"Bushnell is a genius!" Ambrose exclaimed. But his enthusiasm quickly faded as he watched more rowboats come after them. Men stood in the front of their boats and shot at the *Turtle* with their muskets. Fortunately, the submarine appeared to be bulletproof. Ambrose raised his gaze toward the *HMS Lively*. A few of her cannons moved as if being aimed.

"Oh, no. John, the cannons. Can you take us down again?"

John was breathing heavily as he continued to crank the propeller. He hesitated. "I don't think so. I'm exhausted."

Boom.

Ambrose quickly wiped the glass of the porthole and looked out. Black smoke from a cannon filled the air on the side of the ship.

Splash.

The cannonball collided with the water only feet from their vessel.

John looked out the porthole on his side. "We're almost

at the buoy. If we pass it and those rowboats keep coming at us, we're dead."

"If that ship hits us with a cannonball, we're dead too." Ambrose wiped the sweat from his brow. *What to do?* His mind whirring, he glanced around at the controls, then down at the side of the *Turtle*. A rope hung on a peg.

Rope. Yes!

He grabbed it and tied a lasso on the end. He then placed his foot in the rung of the short ladder and unlocked the hinge.

"What are you doing?" John asked, pedaling furiously.

"Helping. At least, I hope. There's no time to connect the planned way."

Ambrose opened the hatch. Fresh air rushed in and he pulled huge gulps of it into his lungs. Splashes from the North River cooled his face. He climbed the small ladder. Half of his body was now exposed to the enemy musket fire.

Bang!

A musket ball *kerplunk*ed into the water behind him, but the enemy was still too far away to aim accurately.

Boom.

The ship's cannon thundered.

Ambrose whirled around to watch in horror. A whistling sound grew louder and louder.

Ker-splash!

The cannonball smashed into the water just ahead of them.

Ambrose spotted the buoy bouncing in the wake near the splash.

"That bomb under the ship should be going off any minute," John's voice called from below. "What if something went wrong?" He stopped pedaling.

Ambrose twirled the rope around and around his head and prayed for steady and accurate aim. He imagined the loop of that rope connecting perfectly with the floating buoy, bobbing in the current, thirty feet from him.

He let the rope fly.

The lasso sailed through the air—and missed.

"What if the powder got wet?" John's voice cracked.

Ka-whoooom.

Ambrose spun around in time to see a huge explosion jolt the British ship. Flames, debris, and black smoke immediately filled the air.

"Yes! Woo-hoo!" Ambrose threw his arm into the air. "Take that as a declaration of independence! There's the answer to your question! We did it, brother!"

Ambrose watched, transfixed, as the giant vessel creaked and cracked. Fire spread outward from its center. Men screamed and ran in every direction on the deck. Some even threw themselves overboard. "It had to be done," Ambrose reminded himself. "Hello, *Lively*." Ambrose declared. "This is the *American Turtle*! The deadly *Turtle*!" The men in the rowboats had stopped and now watched as their flagship creaked and rocked to her side and slowly slipped, foot by foot, into the harbor. Some sailors cried out in terror.

"Ambrose, the rope!" John shouted from below.

Ambrose pulled his rope in and whirled it above his head. It felt heavier now thanks to water on its fibers. He prayed silently and let it sail. Seconds later, it caught the buoy and he pulled it tight. He spun to his right and connected his end of the rope to a steel cleat on the *Turtle*'s outer hull. The *Turtle* moved forward with a jolt, and then skidded on top of the water, heading toward the shoreline.

Shots fired from behind. Musket balls plunked into the river all around them.

More shots were fired, only this time from in front of them.

Ambrose's heart skipped a beat. He reached into the *Turtle*, pulled out his spyglass, and perused his surroundings. Six sharpshooters dressed in coats like fishermen sat in nearby rowboats and fired their long rifles at the Redcoats in the rowboats behind them. Their shots convinced the rowers to keep their distance from the *Turtle*. Ambrose focused on the shoreline where three horses with ropes attached to the buoy pulled the boys closer to the beach.

A man on the beach holding a spyglass waved at him. Ambrose waved back. The horses kept pulling and soon disappeared out of sight down a road. But Ambrose could feel them trudging on as they dragged the *Turtle* through the river.

Ambrose then focused his spyglass on the wagon that had brought the *Turtle* to the shore's edge. Its beams and pulleys with ropes hanging down were ready and waiting for them.

Bushnell thinks of everything.

Ambrose ducked inside the *Turtle*. "We did it, John. The frigate is no more."

"I'm just glad we survived." John sat against the side of the *Turtle*'s tilted hull and caught his breath.

Ambrose rested against the other side of the hull. At the pace the horses were pulling, it would only be a few minutes before they arrived at the shore. "By the way, that buoy and horse-pulling idea of yours was ingenious."

John smiled. "Thanks. It's a good thing you're handy with a lasso like you are with a knife. With those angry Redcoats rowing after us, we wouldn't have had time to connect to it ourselves."

Ambrose breathed deeply and waited for his beating heart to slow. The salt air filled his nostrils. Now that the adrenaline was ebbing, his mind replayed the vision of the fiery ship sinking. Black smoke. Screams.

He sighed.

"What's wrong?" John asked.

"I . . . Um . . . I don't feel like I thought I would."

John paused. "Being a hero and killing the enemy doesn't feel as amazing as you thought it would, does it?"

Ambrose tightened his eyebrows. "No. It doesn't." He looked away and ran his fingers through his damp hair. "I don't feel any better than before." Ambrose swallowed.

"To be honest, I feel numb." He adjusted his weight as the *Turtle* rocked and slowed. He hoped he'd never have to be in harm's way again—or be forced to put someone else there. Life was indeed precious.

"I know how you feel," admitted John. "It didn't feel good shooting that British soldier in his leg either."

Ambrose remembered the incident like it was yesterday. Two Redcoats had chased him, his brother, and father along the Long Island shore and had shot at them. One wounded their father and later hunted him and John down like prey. They beat up John while searching for the spy letter they carried. Fortunately for John, Ambrose went back to find him and was able to throw his knife and stop one of the Redcoats . . . Sergeant Conrad Evans . . . from killing his twin. John then shot the Lobsterback's partner and he had to shoot Evans in the shoulder as well.

"Sometimes, I wonder what became of those Recoats," John admitted.

"They were hanged for their deeds, no doubt," Ambrose speculated. "And rightly so. The world is better off. Enough talk of them. I only hope Berty is all right."

John grew quiet. "Me too," he said at last.

CHAPTER 16

NEW SURROUNDINGS

You're going to be moved to a new location where you will be executed. Hanged on the gallows, traitor."

Berty heard the cutting of the ropes holding his wrists. Seconds later, his limp arms came crashing down from above him and his body hit the floor with a thud.

"Your dead body will sway in the breeze. Our men will spit on you. But your pain will be over." The same voice that belonged to the man who had tortured Berty was cold and distant. "I will give you this . . . you are the most stubborn of the rabble I've ever had the pleasure to beat."

Berty took a breath. His stubbornness had come from his father. He inhaled and exhaled slowly again. One breath at a time. It was all he had focused on. Just keep breathing. And praying. When help did not come . . . nor mercy . . . he had prayed for strength.

His head still covered by the burlap sack, he wondered if he'd ever know what the man who was bruising and beating his body looked like. Or if his family would ever receive his body back or know what had become of him.

CHAPTER 17

BROTHERLY CHALLENGES

Ambrose slid down the outside of the *Turtle* as the sun hung low on the horizon.

"That was astounding!" David Bushnell smiled and extended his arm to help Ambrose. "But we must hurry."

Ambrose's feet sloshed in the water. He turned and caught John as he slid alongside the *Turtle* and gained his footing. A gentle morning breeze blew and swayed the trees along the shoreline. Several men secured ropes to the *Turtle*. Others backed the wagon into the water. More men threaded ropes into pulleys and hoisted the *Turtle* onto the wagon. Fifty feet to the left stood a sleek carriage with a pair of matching brown steeds.

"That's for us." Bushnell motioned Ambrose along the side path. He sniffed. "You boys smell awful."

"Yeah, thanks to your oversized clam back there." John

shook his head like a dog and water sprayed around him. "That is just sweat. Is my change of clothes in that carriage?"

"Yes," Bushnell answered. He turned to Ambrose. "Yours too."

Feeling ecstatic to be back safely on land, Ambrose gripped the inventor's shoulder. "Let me tell you something, sir. That *Turtle* of yours certainly did snap."

Bushnell grinned. "Yes, she did. Thank you for proving my vision could work." Bushnell paused. "What was it like?"

Ambrose stopped in his tracks and locked eyes with the American tinkerer. He took a deep breath and paused thoughtfully. "Tiring." He walked slowly up the bank to the carriage.

"I was expecting a different description," Bushnell called after him, "but I understand."

"Your fungus worked too!" John shouted as he lumbered up the small hill to join his brother.

Ambrose climbed onto the back of the carriage. "That just doesn't sound right."

John laughed and uneasily maneuvered his body aboard. Both boys took an arm and helped Mr. Bushnell into the vehicle. The inventor fell onboard, almost ending up in Ambrose's lap. Ambrose scooted toward the center of the back seat.

Bushnell took a cushion from the corner of the carriage and placed it under his bottom. "We're going to a safe place to rest in Hackensack, New Jersey." The tinkerer took a deep breath and his expression grew serious. "I have news from Major Tallmadge."

Ambrose leaned closer to the inventor. Was it about Berty? His heartbeat sped up.

Bushnell swallowed and found his voice. "First, the major informed me that the Stocking gunpowder factory has been destroyed."

"What?" exclaimed Ambrose, sitting back.

Bushnell nodded grimly. "It exploded. George Senior, two sons, and two workers perished. Only one son and wife and the head of security are still alive. They were not home when the tragedy occurred."

Ambrose looked down at the carriage's floor. He had only met Mr. Stocking the one time, but he seemed like such a brave and noble man—and an invaluable patriot.

"How did it happen?" asked John.

"Apparently an accident . . ." Bushnell shook his head. "There was an electrical storm in the area. But Tallmadge thinks otherwise."

"Foul play?" Ambrose's mouth hung open. The Redcoats and Loyalists would surely want it gone . . . if they knew about it.

"Possibly," Bushnell paused and looked down. When he looked up again, his eyes were brighter. "Now, for the better news. The Culper spies discovered that your brother Berty and the other prisoners are alive—" Ambrose's heart leapt—"but they are being moved to a place called Fort Saint George on Long Island to be hanged. The Loyalists who captured your brother also brought the kegs of gunpowder there. The good major and his Dragoons are planning to attack in two days." Bushnell leaned in. "Tallmadge gave the British false information. If they believe it, they are expecting him to land on another part of the island. That will force the British to use many of their troops to defend that area. And fewer men will be in the fort."

Hanged. Ambrose couldn't get that word out of his mind. His stomach clenched at the thought of his brother with a noose around his neck. He'd never forgive the men behind his brother's capture. "If he's going after our brother, we should join them," Ambrose's sense of duty was met quickly by inner questions. He struggled to find his next words. If he and John joined Tallmadge, things could go wrong. One or both of them could die. He was mortal after all. And he certainly didn't want to put himself in a position where he might have to kill more people—somebody's sons. But this was Berty . . .

"Ambrose, I understand how you feel," John said. "But maybe this is one thing we should leave to Ben Tallmadge and his soldiers."

A short, plump man jumped into the driver's seat and took the reins.

Bushnell whistled, and their carriage moved forward. "Look at you both. You're exhausted," Bushnell said. "You're in no shape to—"

"But he's my brother." Ambrose watched the horses pull

the *Turtle*'s wagon out of the water. "*Our* brother. Right, John?" He turned to his twin.

John fidgeted and looked the other way. "Ambrose, he's right." He reached for the carriage's side rail. "Stop feeling like you need to risk your own neck. Major Tallmadge and his men can handle it. We'll just get in the way."

Ambrose bounced in his seat as the carriage bumped down the road. Was John being a coward? No. Just practical, as always. But something deep inside of Ambrose was telling him to go. However, maybe for the first time in his life, a big part of himself fought that feeling. He should be more practical, like John. Stay safe. Yet, he had learned so much about himself since they placed the letter in George Washington's hand and now, since he piloted the *Turtle*. Why couldn't he build on that? He felt afraid—terrified actually. But something was still telling him to go. "That's not what I'm feeling at all," he said to John.

John kicked at his brother's leg from where he sat across from him. "We just sank a British warship! I'm wet. Tired. Hungry. I smell bad and I need sleep."

Ambrose kicked John back. "So eat some biscuits! You're cranky."

"I agree with John." Bushnell grabbed hold of the railing as the carriage hit a bumpy stretch of road. "I shouldn't have said anything."

A hawk circled above in the morning sky. Ambrose rode silently for a few minutes watching it. If he did nothing and left it to Tallmadge and his men and they failed, he could never live with himself. But if he tried and failed . . . at least he had done something. Maybe they would succeed . . . with God's help. The urge to do this was powerful. Was God speaking to him? Ambrose turned to John and said, "Look . . . I'm tired too. I want to go home, but this is our brother. I'm sad about the Stockings and the men that died." He looked at Bushnell. "But I'm glad you told us. And I don't want to risk my life or your life, John. "

John opened his mouth to speak, but Ambrose continued. "I just feel like . . . I feel like I'm *supposed* to be there. That's all." He paused. "My little voice is telling me to go." He focused his eyes on John. "And if you be still, I bet you'll hear it too."

"Little voice?" Bushnell asked.

"You might call it your conscience," Ambrose said.

Bushnell nodded. "Some might call it Providential spirit," Bushnell declared. "I understand."

Ambrose looked into his brother's eyes. "It's telling me to go."

John sighed. "I'm not hearing anything now . . . except for this uncomfortable carriage clunking down the road!" His voice rose.

Ambrose turned to Mr. Bushnell. "He is cranky."

"Better cranky than stupid." John's eyes closed.

Ambrose shook his head. He glanced at his rucksack sitting beside him. His eyebrows raised. He reached inside and pulled out his fife.

"Really?" John asked. "You're going to play that now?"

Ambrose put the fife to his lips and played a few fast notes just to annoy his brother.

Bushnell grinned at Ambrose's musical ability.

Ambrose sighed. If his brother would agree to help, and if Berty was still alive, he knew how he'd use his fife next.

CHAPTER 18

LOOKING BACK
AND AHEAD

He strolled alone quietly through the forest a mile from Fort St. George. His three prisoners of war had been delivered. Soon, they would hang.

The sky wasn't as gray or the air as damp but the woods reminded him of his boyhood home back in England. He'd often run through the trees playing tag with his brother Charles, who was three years younger. That was before pneumonia took the lives of his mother and father. He and his brother had then been placed in an orphanage.

He ran away from the life of an orphan at fifteen and found work on a merchant ship. The life of a sailor had been harsh. But he was thankful for his year at sea, where he learned how to keep decks spotless and hundreds of words that would make any average man blush.

From there, he joined His Majesty's Royal Army, the

most powerful force in the world. He was never hungry or lonely in the military. And he was always busy learning new ways to lead men and get the best out of them. His natural intelligence and cunning were both qualities his superiors recognized and made use of to the fullest.

A purple flower blooming in his path caught his eye. He randomly remembered his mother loving flowers. Strange. He hadn't thought about her in years. Why now? He'd seen flowers before and even appreciated their beauty.

If only his mother . . .

Rubbish.

He brushed the thought and emotion aside.

He had been a teenager when he set out on his own. And now he'd been charged with spying on two teens. Soon, his mission—and their lives—would be over, and he'd move on to another member of the Clark family, perhaps Enoch or Lamberton. Yes, the father would be ideal to focus on next.

Now those twin boys had managed to do what no one else could—sink a British frigate in a strange contraption.

He'd known about the Continental's *Turtle* for over a year, of course. His informants and spies had told him about Bushnell's invention long ago. So how had they succeeded when the others hadn't?

The local tavern keeper in Old Saybrook was also the postmaster, and a secret Loyalist. He had been opening Bushnell's correspondence, reading it, and sharing his plans with the British for a long time now.

He laughed silently to himself.

If only the two boys were on His Majesty's side. He could use them.

His only son had skills too, even better ones than the Clark boys and each one of his son's accomplishments using those abilities made him proud. The young man was more like he than his mother. But his wife was lovely and loyal to the king. He couldn't wait to see her again. Soon enough, he assured himself.

Too bad, Lamberton, old chap. You and your family are on the wrong side.

He plucked the flower, brought it up to his nose, and smelled it. He didn't know how to describe the smell nor could he identify the plant. No matter. Yes, the man's thoughts wandered again. When they won this war, he'd go back to England and try to find his brother. His mother would have liked that. Surely he had survived the orphanage and was a businessman somewhere. He had the same ambitious blood running through his veins after all.

CHAPTER 19

UNTIL A BETTER TIME

What do you mean Tallmadge postponed his plans?" Ambrose set down his cup of tea and tried to gain control over the sudden emotions that threatened to choke him.

"That's what he said in his message." Bushnell shrugged, his eyes sad. "A courier rode all night to deliver it."

"Let me see that, please." John respectfully held out his hand to take the letter from the *Turtle* inventor, and Bushnell handed it over.

Ambrose got up from his chair and stood behind John. It read exactly as Bushnell stated. But was this a diversion by Tallmadge so the twins wouldn't get involved? Tallmadge, after all, was a master of strategy and cunning. Certainly he wouldn't deceive a family friend, especially in a matter as important as a rescue attempt. Or would he?

"Until a better time," John read. "They're not going now? When's a better time? After Berty's dead?"

John's gaze locked on his brother. His face was like stone.

Ambrose knew his twin was now fully committed to a rescue attempt of their own. He glanced around at his surroundings in the sitting room at the inn. The light blue walls reminded him of Berty' bedroom. He had to do whatever it took to help. He felt it deep within himself. Although he didn't understand the tug on his heart, he knew he had to listen to it. He didn't want to risk his life again, ever. Since piloting the *Turtle* and killing so many men, he had seen enough death, and he didn't want to die young. But this was Berty. Could he muster up the courage again to do what needed to be done when the time came? He hoped so.

"Did you see this?" John pointed. "Tallmadge says we need to remember the war isn't just about Berty."

"He's right," Bushnell said gently. "But I am terribly sorry about your brother." He held out his hand to take the letter back.

"We understand," Ambrose replied. "I guess we'll just have to be patient and let Tallmadge and his men handle this when he thinks it best."

John stared at his brother suspiciously. Ambrose knew John didn't believe those words.

Ambrose's eyes told his brother more. They would make their own plans. Certainly the grownups wouldn't approve. But if they could successfully get a message to General Washington and blow up an enemy ship in a submarine, surely they could find the fort and try to rescue their brother. He glanced at Bushnell. Did the Yankee tinkerer believe him? He'd bet his last coin that he did. His thoughts turned to the dangers that lay ahead. He only hoped his mother wouldn't soon be mourning the loss of three sons instead of possibly one.

I don't want to die, Lord. Please be with us.

CHAPTER 20

ALWAYS TOGETHER

A torrential downpour pelted Ambrose's tar-coated sailing jacket. Gusts of wind rushed across the Sound, threatening to toss his broad-brimmed hat into the sea. Ambrose held onto it with one hand. "Aren't you glad you listened to that little voice?" he called to his brother.

"No! Not really!" John held onto the rail of the sailboat and looked a little sick.

Ambrose grinned.

After thanking Mr. Bushnell for his hospitality and an amazing adventure, Ambrose told the inventor he and his brother needed to take care of some business. Ambrose was convinced the Yankee tinkerer didn't suspect they would attempt to rescue Berty on their own, but knowing how intelligent the man was, he knew Bushnell probably suspected the boys were up to something.

Ambrose and John had mapped out their plan. When the boys arrived at Fort St. George, they would claim they were from Staten Island, sailing on a sloop in the Atlantic Ocean, when the wind snapped their mast. They washed ashore and had come to the fort seeking safety. What adult, even a British soldier or Loyalist, could turn away two soaking-wet, shivering, and scared boys? None, he hoped.

Ambrose was used to sailing in the rain. The extra-strong wind gusts and high waves worried him, but he never showed John his concern. He aimed the boat for the shore and once the hull brushed onto the sand, he dropped the sail. Ambrose jumped into the water, followed by John. They grabbed hold of the wet, cold hull and dragged the small, borrowed sailboat onto the shore away from the waves. John put down the mast, and they hid the boat in the reeds. The fort was too far away for anyone to check their broken mast story. Not in this weather anyway.

With no weapon except his knife, Ambrose didn't know how they were going to rescue their brother or even if he was still there or alive. Was he worried?

Yes. Something could go extremely wrong as he tried to save their brother, but there was something else. Something he didn't fully understand. It left a haunting feeling.

"Let's go!" Ambrose shouted to John as the wind howled around them. Fortunately, the rain had slowed to a drizzle.

Yeah, now the rain stops. Why not an hour ago, when we were fighting the waves and squalls?

He took his compass from his satchel and waited a

moment for the needle to gain its magnetic direction. It steadied. "Good. We go this way." Ambrose closed the wooden compass box, flicked the brass clasp locking it, and thrust it inside his bag. Finally, draping the satchel strap over his shoulder, he gave John a nod. Together they began walking southeast, away from the beach.

The brothers trekked for several miles across Long Island. The terrain switched from sand to grassy knolls to marshes and finally to woods. When the rain stopped completely, Ambrose took off his hat and shoved it into his satchel. As they continued walking, he replayed in his mind the events of the *Turtle* approaching the British frigate.

Why did that sailor say those words? *"There it is."* Not *"What is that?"* Surely anyone seeing the *Turtle* or even the top of it for the first time would say, *"What is that?"*

Unless the sailor saw the other *Turtle*s too . . . But what were the chances? *Turtles* had only attacked a handful of ships. Ambrose's gut tightened. He looked at John. "I've been thinking: we're lucky we blew that ship up and got out of there alive. They were looking for us. Expecting us."

John stopped and opened the canteen that hung from a strap on his shoulder. "Luck had nothing to do with it. Providence did."

"Yes, I know." Ambrose nodded impatiently. "But the British seem to have spies too. And I believe one may be close to us. There are too many coincidences."

He reached out his hand. John handed him the canteen, and Ambrose took a drink.

John said, "There have been way too many people shooting at us."

"Ah." Ambrose wiped his mouth with his hand. "True." He handed the canteen back to his brother. "I have a confession to make."

Confused, John looked over at his brother.

"I knew all along—even from the moment I volunteered—that you'd be in the *Turtle* with me."

John wrinkled his brow.

"I knew you couldn't let me do it alone. Like Dad said, you're the one who always looks after me." Ambrose looked at the sun breaking through the grey clouds. "I wasn't as brave as they thought. I wasn't sure if I could handle it, and I was really hoping you'd say you wanted in."

John took another swig of water, then eyed him. "I almost *did* let you do it alone."

"No. I couldn't have done it without you."

John smiled. "I know." He threw the strap of the canteen back over his shoulder.

Ambrose opened his satchel and took out a hand-drawn map of the area and the fort's location that he received from a patriot before they left New Jersey. "Well, I hope Dad is having good luck finding the traitor who told the British about him. I have a feeling all of this is connected." He glanced at the map. "If this is accurate, the British fort should soon be in sight."

The twins changed direction and headed south. They hiked over a ridge, and there it was—Fort St. George. Large walls of vertical twelve-foot logs told visitors this was not an ordinary village. Looking down on it, the twins could see the walls formed a triangle, attached in the back to a square manor house. In front of the walls, a stockade with sharpened branches pointed outward, surrounded by a deep ditch. This all would certainly slow down any army.

John knelt next to his twin. "He's in there. I feel it."

"Yeah, me too." Ambrose gazed at the fort, at the few figures moving around. "Glad you came even though your little voice wasn't screaming at you like mine."

"It's becoming a bad habit of mine. But this is the last time. After today, I'm going home to Connecticut. Eating mother's pie by a warm fire. Not leaving the house for days."

"Not even to visit Sophie?" Ambrose took a deep breath and purposefully didn't add, "If we make it out of this fort alive."

"No. Not even for that."

With a sigh, Ambrose gently punched John's shoulder. "Okay. Act casual. Innocent. We have to be believable." He thought about his plan. It seemed like it could actually work. The thought made him feel slightly better.

"You're right, brother," John took a breath. As he exhaled, a look of confidence appeared on his face. Seeing it gave Ambrose a jolt as well. John added, "We are acting. Not lying. At least that's what I tell myself."

Ambrose stretched his arms. "We are on the side of right. Don't forget that." He paused. "It will help you act better."

The twins stood up and approached the fort side by side.

They were in full view, no more than twenty feet from the fence, when an armed sentry shouted from the top of the wooden barrier, "Who goes there?"

Ambrose stopped walking and took a deep breath. "We're from Staten Island!" he called.

"We were on our sloop in the Atlantic—" John said tearfully.

"When the wind snapped our mast!" Ambrose finished. He tried to sound pitiful.

"We washed ashore and came here seeking safety!" Good. John sounded weary. And scared.

He probably is.

"Please, we're cold, tired . . ."

"And hungry," Ambrose cried out. "Can you help us?"

The sentry hesitated and shifted his weight nervously.

"If you can't help, is there somewhere else close we can go for help?"

Good one, John. We all know the answer to that one. No.

"No," the sentry replied. "Is there anyone else with you?"

"It's just us," Ambrose answered. He nodded to John.

The sentry paused, as if studying the brothers. "You boys look exactly alike."

Ambrose shook his head. "We're twins." He added under his breath, "Genius."

"Umm . . . all right. Proceed!" The sentry motioned with his musket toward the front gate.

The twins followed the direction he pointed. John glanced at the line-up of sharp timber facing them. "I wouldn't want to run into those."

"That would ruin your day," Ambrose agreed.

Krrrrr-thud. A wooden plank was removed from behind the gate. Seconds later the gate swung open. Another sentry, a short man with a bulbous nose, appeared, his musket aimed at John. "You boys look awful." He lowered his musket.

"Thanks a lot," John muttered.

Ambrose elbowed him. "Sorry, sir. He's just cranky." He turned to the sentry. "Thank you for helping us. We just need to get dry and get something to eat and drink."

"And a little rest," John added.

"Then maybe someone can help us get back to Staten Island." Ambrose tried to look helpless.

At the man's gesture, the twins walked inside. Another soldier closed the gate and slid the plank into position. They were locked inside the fort.

A shiver ran down Ambrose's spine. *I felt safer in the* Turtle. He faced an open courtyard. Three tall wooden walls protected the fort. Inside were several buildings. Bunkhouses, weapons depots, storage areas, a mess hall, and officers' quarters, no doubt.

The sentry grabbed Ambrose's satchel and searched it. Finding nothing of interest, he grunted and pushed it into Ambrose's chest. "You're in luck. The patrol isn't back yet. Must have gotten caught in the same storm as you. You can use a couple of their bunks." The sentry led them across the compound with short strides.

Ambrose stopped. To his right stood three platforms and nooses for a hanging. "What's that?"

"Oh, that." The sentry jerked a nod. "There's no real prison here. But three hostages are being kept in a locked room under heavy guard. Later today they'll be hanged as traitors."

"Good." Ambrose started up again, faster this time.

John followed by his side. "Traitors *should* be hanged."

The sentry led the twins to a bunkhouse where several beds lined the walls. In the next room, three large dining tables and chairs sat in the center.

"All we have for you is some bread." The sentry walked away. "It might be a little stale, but it's edible."

"We'll take it," John said gratefully.

"I wonder if stale Redcoat bread is any good," Ambrose whispered. He glanced around the room. "This isn't very homey." Bare, plank walls looked back at him. Even a painting of the king hanging on a wall would have been better than nothing. A few trunks of clothing flanked several beds.

The sentry brought the twins a jug of fresh spring water, two cups, and the loaf of bread, as promised. After they finished eating, Ambrose opened his satchel and pulled out his fife. He knew exactly the tune he would play—and play loudly. Loud enough so when Berty heard it, he'd know his brothers were close by.

"You can play that thing?" the sentry asked.

"No, I just thought I'd scratch my back with it." Ambrose smiled playfully at the Redcoat. "Of course I can play it." Ambrose guessed the man was in his early thirties and, by the size of his protruding belly, out of shape.

"You better be good or I'll have to turn you over to the Continentals." The sentry grinned sarcastically in return. His teeth were a disaster.

"Wouldn't want that to happen." Ambrose placed the fife to his lips and blew. The tune of *A Mighty Fortress* floated through the building as Ambrose's fingertips danced up and down the fife.

Help is near, Berty. I hope you can hear this.

Ambrose sang the lyrics to the song in his mind. The music from the fife, combined with his inner singing, lifted his spirits. It appeared to have the same effect on the sentry, who leaned his musket against the wall and relaxed.

Ambrose grinned. *It seems my music calmed the savage Redcoat.*

He winked at John, who looked wistful himself. With the last note still echoing through the room, Ambrose took the fife away from his lips and scratched his back with it.

The sentry chuckled. John rolled his eyes.

Before anyone could speak, a loud whistle—sounding like *"Wee-r-up!"*—rang in reply to the music. Ambrose's heart leapt and he looked at John in relief.

He's alive! And he knows we are here.

CHAPTER 21

SURPRISES

John nodded at Ambrose and grinned. He looked just as relieved as Ambrose felt.

The sentry had straightened when he heard the whistle. Now he looked quizzically at Ambrose, his gaze sharpening. Obviously, he sensed from the twins' reaction that something fishy was going on.

"Hey—" He stepped toward Ambrose.

Jumping up, John grabbed the soldier's musket, but before he could point it, the sentry kicked it out of his hand and he was hurled heavily to the ground.

Ambrose grabbed the Brit by the shoulders and tried to pry him off his brother but the young man elbowed him in the stomach and smashed John in the face with a left hook.

Ambrose lunged at the man knocking him off his brother.

Smack—smash—smack!

Ambrose delivered three blows in swift succession.

The sentry propelled Ambrose off him with a push of his legs. He stood up and before he knew it, John smashed the man in the back of his head with the butt of his own musket. The sentry wobbled. John kicked his legs out from under him, helping him fall faster and harder. In just a second, the Brit lay unconscious on the dirt floor.

Ambrose gaped at John. "Thank you. You are brave, brother."

With a shaky grin and shrug, John put the musket on the table and reached into his brother's bag. He pulled out some rope and wrapped it around the Redcoat's hands. "Yeah, I amaze myself sometimes."

Ambrose raced to the window, yanked a cord from a curtain, returned to the man to tie his feet. He pulled his knot tight, then ran into the bunkroom, snatched a sheet, and ripped it to make a gag for the man.

"Does your face hurt? That was a pretty good punch," Ambrose asked, concerned.

"It actually just grazed me. Stings, but I'm fine." The twins carried the gagged Redcoat to a bed and covered him with a sheet.

"Anyone just glancing in will think he's asleep," John said with a small grin.

Ambrose dusted his hands, wiping them on his shirt as if touching a British soldier made him feel dirty. "He'll have a *Turtle*-sized headache for sure later."

John had snatched the musket off the table and now held it in both hands. He smiled.

Ambrose looked at John's musket. "Keep your eyes open for another one of those."

"Yes, I think you'll need one."

Ambrose touched the rough leather handle of his knife, which nestled inside a case on the back of his belt. He was glad he knew how to use the knife, if needed. He ran towards the door and opened it a crack. Four men ambled across the courtyard. He gently closed the door.

John whispered over Ambrose's shoulder, "Berty's whistle came from that direction." He pointed to the back of the fortress.

Ambrose slowly opened the door again. "He said there was a heavy guard, so take a casual stroll that way and look for an area where there are men guarding a door."

John looked at his brother. "Me?"

"Yeah, just leave the musket."

"I don't want to be the one to go. Why don't you do it?"

Ambrose sighed in disgust, "Fine."

Two men dressed as civilians in britches and coats strolled by on the other side of the yard. Ambrose opened the door and stepped outside. He stood still and watched. They paid him no mind. Ambrose stretched and yawned then pushed his legs forward.

Just be casual and act like you belong. You're harmless. You didn't just blow up a British warship.

He nodded at a tall, thin, red-headed man who pushed a wheelbarrow loaded with rocks.

You aren't here to rescue your patriot brother. You're just a kid walking around inside an enemy fort.

He strolled to a section of the fortress that had a window with bars on it. Yes, he decided. This could be a place where they would keep undesirables—undesirables like Berty. Sure enough, by the front door, a heavy man sat on a stool with a musket on his lap.

Ambrose held back a laugh. Apparently, when the sentry said a heavy guard, he meant a fat guard, not multiple men.

He walked by a wooden cart, then smiled and waved at the guard as he neared. *Don't worry, I'm not here to hurt you or rescue my brother.If only I had some sweet cakes and muffins to tempt you away with.*

Ambrose lifted his chin in a nod. "Hi."

The heavy soldier smiled at him.

"What's in there?"

"Prisoners."

"Wow! Real prisoners?" Ambrose took a step back.

"These prisoners are going to be hanged this afternoon . . . as soon as the patrol gets back."

Ambrose widened his eyes. "I'm glad they're in there and I'm out here. Keep up the great work." Acting nervous, he turned on his heel. Then, cracking a smile, he whistled *A Mighty Fortress* as loudly as he could as he headed back for John.

As Ambrose approached the barracks, the door slowly opened. "Did you find them?" John whispered.

"Yes." Ambrose slipped inside. "Now all we need is some kind of a—"

A musket shot rang out. Followed by another. And shouts from men.

"Diversion?" John finished his brother's sentence.

Heart pounding, Ambrose paused and listened to more gunfire. Could they be caught in the middle of a battle? What was happening? His stomach fluttered.

"Tallmadge?" John gave his brother a quizzical look.

More musket fire came from outside the compound. Could the major have lied to them?

In front of the twins, men ran to the manor house in response to the shooting. Another man dashed from the house, pulling his red uniform coat on as he darted to a ladder that led to the platform at the top of the fence.

Ambrose's pulse quickened. He could hear men yelling from all three sides of the stockade. He looked up and saw members of the Second Continental Light Dragoons coming over the top of one of the three fences.

"For Washington and glory!" a man shouted from the top of the barricade.

His words were met with the exact watchwords from the second fence, "For Washington and glory!"

"For Washington and glory!" came the echo from the third barricade wall.

It was an awe-inspiring moment, and a chill ran down Ambrose's spine. He had never been more proud to be a Patriot. "He was decoying us with that letter. Why that—" Ambrose shook his head, then realized, "We should help him." Ambrose opened the door, then hesitated.

"What's wrong?" John asked.

"We could die . . . out there . . . in a matter of moments."

John placed his hand on his brother's shoulder, as more gunfire blasted throughout the compound. He looked his brother in the eye. "So far, all your plans have worked out. I trust you . . . and I have your back. You can depend on me. We'll do this together like always." John gave his brother a nod.

A battle had begun outside. Ambrose had to act fast. He took a deep breath. "Thanks, brother." He took another deep breath and steeled his nerves. "For Washington, Berty, and glory."

John slapped his brother on the back.

Ambrose bolted through the doorway and ran to the main gate. John was right by his side. At the top of the fence, puff after puff of black smoke rose into the air from British muskets firing at attackers on the outside. The twins grabbed hold of the heavy wooden plank hanging on the gate and heaved it back through the lock. It dropped onto the ground. Ambrose swung open the gate. Seconds later, a flood of militiamen burst through, weapons raised and shouting.

A volley of musketry fired at the patriot invaders from windows of the manor house. A musket ball whizzed past Ambrose's head.

Major Tallmadge appeared over the fence on the right, his musket strapped over his shoulder. He hit the ground, stood up, and positioned his weapon firmly in his grasp.

His determined eyes were fixed on the building and musket fire ahead of him. "Break down the doors with axes, men!" The major turned and spotted Ambrose and John. His eyes fell on the twins and widened in shock.

Feeling the weight of Tallmadge's gaze, Ambrose turned to John. "Time to get Berty and the others."

John nodded and the two sprinted towards Berty's prison as the major crushed an attacker with the butt of his musket and forged ahead into battle. Ambrose dodged a pile of loose rocks and was halfway to the door when—

"Unnhhh!"

Ambrose whirled around. John lay on the ground, grimacing in pain. Shot? Ambrose's heart leaped to his throat. A prayer on his lips, he raced to his brother's side. John groaned and clutched his ankle.

"Are you wounded?" Ambrose examined his brother's legs for signs of blood.

With a grimace, John rolled up his right trouser leg. His ankle was already beginning to swell. "I tripped on those loose rocks back there. It's a bad sprain, I can tell."

Musket fire thundered around them. Ambrose quickly placed his arm around his twin and hauled him to a nearby building. He hoped it would offer at least some protection from the battle.

John rested against the wall and rubbed his ankle. "I can't believe this! How stupid of me!" He tried to get up, but when he put weight on his foot, he collapsed.

Ambrose breathed heavily. "What are we going to do?"

He tried to think, but the gunfire and screams all around them made his brain move sluggishly. Finally, he stopped and looked at John.

His brother nodded. "You have to rescue Berty," he said softly.

Ambrose wrung his hands. "I don't want to leave you. We've done everything together. Two are stronger."

"You can do this without me." John grimaced as he shifted his weight. "The harder the conflict . . ."

Ambrose paused, remembering Washington's words. "The . . . more glorious the triumph." He stared a long moment at his brother. "Okay." Ambrose took the musket. "But you just don't sit here. Pray."

Ambrose got to his feet and took stock of the scene. Men fought man-to-man with bayonets. Volleys of musket fire rang out between the British and the Dragoons. Ambrose darted to a corner of the stockade and hid beside a wooden cart. Twenty feet to his right stood the plump guard, a worried look frozen on the Redcoat's face. He held his musket ready to fire. Ambrose could tell he wanted to get into the action. He looked ready to abandon his post.

Between Ambrose and the guard, Patriots fought Loyalists and Redcoats. If only he could get through them unharmed. He remembered Cooper at the gunpowder factory. Think and move like a cat. Ambrose imagined himself doing so. He darted ahead and scooted past a patriot in a bayonet fight with a Lobsterback. He wanted to help the young soldier but kept moving ahead swiftly past combatants, weaving through the fighting. He raced past a Dragoon who had been shot in the leg and lay in pain on the ground as the man who shot him ran toward Ambrose. He raised his weapon to fire. Suddenly, another Dragoon ran in front of him and slashed his bayonet against the Redcoat's with a thrust and a parry and stabbed him in the chest. Ambrose kept running sure-footedly, his destination only feet away. *Thank you, Cooper.* Maybe someday he'd see him again and tell him about this.

Ambrose ran up to the anxious guard, raising his one hand and holding the musket toward the sky to show he wasn't shooting. "I'm safe . . . You're needed on the east fence." It wasn't hard to make his voice sound breathless with urgency. "My uncle is one of the commanding officers here. Go. I'll stand guard for you."

Shots and screams echoed behind them.

The guard didn't say a word but ran to assist his comrades.

Ambrose waited until the guard was out of sight then smashed the lock with the butt of his musket. It fell open with a clank. He kicked in the door.

Berty was huddled by the side window. Crouched next to him was Joshua and another colonial prisoner, watching the action. They spun to face him. Berty grinned. His face was black and blue, and one eye was swollen shut. Joshua and the other man had similar wounds. The soldier looked hopeful when he saw that Ambrose wasn't wearing a red jacket or pointing a musket at them. "Well, if it isn't my favorite fifer." Crossing the room, Berty briefly wrapped his arms around his brother. "I heard the music."

Ambrose held Berty tightly. "I heard the whistle."

"Where's John?"

Ambrose stepped back and gestured over his shoulder. "Back there. He sprained his ankle. It looks bad."

Berty nodded and motioned for his fellow Patriots to follow.

Joshua hobbled up to Ambrose. "Thank you," he said, putting a hand on his arm.

Ambrose nodded at Joshua. He'd lead them back toward John, then find a safe place to hide in the fort or a way outside to safety. "This way!" He waved them out then scurried ahead to the side of the fence behind a woodpile. With the men behind him, he made eye contact with John who now stood at the side of a nearby building.

Tallmadge's men stood in the center of the compound. They had already secured several Redcoats and Loyalists who had dropped their guns on the ground in surrender. Two dead Redcoats lay a few feet away from Ambrose. Musket fire, screams, and shouting still echoed around them.

John limped toward him. Ambrose threw his musket back to him. Suddenly, a Redcoat came out of a building with musket in hand. As he lifted his weapon to fire at John, Ambrose, as quick as a striking snake, secured his knife and sent it soaring through the air. It stuck in the Lobsterback's forearm. The man screamed and dropped his weapon. Gunfire from a Dragoon pierced the man's chest and sent him to the ground with a thud. Not wasting a moment, Ambrose bent down and scooped up a musket from the closest dead Redcoat. He tossed it to Berty, who snatched it from the air. Ambrose ran to one of the other dead men and pried the weapon from his hands. *Too much death. Why couldn't the British just leave the colonies alone?* He looked back at his brothers. He had to get Berty out of here. He'd do whatever it took to make sure his brothers went home to their mother.

Several more musket shots filled the air. Ambrose crouched down a little and ran back to the shelter of the woodpile. More than forty wounded Loyalist soldiers moaned throughout the complex. About fifteen more fired on the Dragoons from different strategic areas on the left, right, and center of the compound.

From behind the woodpile, Joshua saluted Ambrose then staggered across the courtyard as fast as his injured body allowed, rolled on the ground, and scooped up a dead British soldier's musket in one swift movement. Using its bayonet, he joined the fighting. Berty's other prison mate ran toward the front gate and disappeared into the woods.

Ambrose slid John's arm across his shoulders. The two hobbled, side by side, toward another nearby shed for protection, Berty beside them. The gunpowder was in the weapons room near the front of the fort. Tallmadge would have it secured in no time. He pointed toward the manor house. They'd head there next. Ambrose nodded to Berty and, supporting John, they moved as fast as they could in that direction.

Suddenly, John tripped and fell out of Ambrose's grasp. His musket landed in the dirt several feet away from him. Berty dropped his own musket beside John and knelt down to help him up.

"You!" a voice snarled from behind him.

Ambrose spun around. His mouth fell open and his heart skipped a beat. Conrad Evans, the British Redcoat who had shot his father, was standing not twenty feet away from him, his black and white horse whinnied from behind the soldier. His weapon pointed directly at Ambrose's head.

Ambrose struggled to find words. "But . . . you were handed over to General Washington. How can you be here?"

"Prisoner exchange. Two weeks later. You see, I am quite valuable to my side." the Redcoat sneered. "I had to learn to use my other hand, thanks to you. But you'll see momentarily I am as good a shot with this one as with the other."

From the corner of his eye, Ambrose saw Berty's hand creep closer to his musket.

"You have no honor," Ambrose said softly. "Prisoners in exchanges vow to give up the fight and return home for the gift of their lives and freedom."

"The only honor I take is in killing traitors." Evans locked his gaze on the twins. "Did you enjoy knowing we had your brother? I hope you suffered. I intended to kill you both someday soon. Your being here only advances my plans more quickly. I regret you will not suffer for long."

John fumbled in the dirt for a rock.

Ambrose started to raise his gun, but stopped when the Redcoat took a step closer to him.

Evans pointed his weapon at Ambrose and Berty. "You both have guns from my comrades. How do you know they haven't already been fired?" the British sergeant snickered. "I will take great pride in killing all three of you. After I shoot one of you, I think I'll kill the others with my bayonet," he planned out loud.

Ambrose placed his finger on the trigger. His spine prickled. The blood of the men on the warship was already on his hands. Could he kill again? He hesitated.

Berty grabbed his weapon. A shot rang out from somewhere behind them, followed by another.

Ambrose pulled his trigger. Nothing happened. His weapon was empty. But it made no difference. Blood spurted from the chest of the Redcoat before him at the same time that Evans' gun fired. Ambrose gasped.

"Unhhh!"

Ambrose spun around. John was grabbing his right arm above his bicep. Blood soaked his shirtsleeve. Gray smoke billowed from Berty's musket. "You can't delay in battle." He pointed his finger at Ambrose then ran to John's side.

Conrad Evans fell to his knees. Ambrose's pulse raced. His face felt hot. The blast from Berty's musket had wounded the Redcoat, causing his aim to falter and shoot John. He ran at the Brit with the butt of his musket raised, ready to smash the enemy's face. The man had caused his twin enough pain and he was behind Berty's capture. Now it was his turn to suffer as well. But Evans collapsed to the ground. Ambrose stepped briskly toward the Brit. Blood spread over the Lobsterback's shirt. He would not live. Of that he was certain. What did John say earlier about forgiveness? It had to be given. Surely this man didn't care if he was forgiven or not. But if he didn't forgive him, he wouldn't be forgiven for his wrongdoings as well. That was a hard teaching. Ambrose stood over Evans and felt the anger inside him ebb a little.

The soldier fell to his side. His hat rolled in the dirt. Blood gurgled from his chest and seeped into the ground. Ambrose knelt beside him.

"You're traitors . . . all of you." The Redcoat coughed.

Ambrose sighed. "No." He took the weapon from the soldier's grasp. "We're Sons of Liberty . . . not traitors." He locked eyes with the dying man.

The soldier took his last breath.

Ambrose's eyes filled with tears. He actually felt pity for the man. Only God knew the kind of life Evans had lived. No one's life was always easy. Ambrose took stock of his surroundings. Ben Tallmadge and his men had finally secured the fort. The battle was over . . . in so many ways.

He looked down at the dead Redcoat. *This is for me as much as it is you.* In his heart, he took a moment to forgive the man who shot his father. Ambrose gazed at his lifeless body. He had never been so close to a dying man.

The soldier's hat rolled in the wind. Ambrose picked it up. Something inside the brim caught his attention: *CREVANS*.

The name was burned inside the brim of the hat. But this man's name was Evans—

Ahh . . . Sergeant Conrad Evans.

Gripping the hat firmly in his hand, he slowly stood up and looked at his brothers.

"It's just a flesh wound!" Berty said to his brother as he wrapped a piece of his shirt around John's arm. "He'll be all right!"

Now I understand why I felt I had to do this. Ambrose marched toward his brothers with intense eyes. Ambrose held up the hat for John to see.

"*CREVANS*," John read. "*C-R-EVANS*. That means the man who shot dad was also at the Stocking's gunpowder factory that night."

"Yes . . . Evans was also a spy." Ambrose nodded at the Brit. "He must have been told about Dad's mission. That's how they discovered him and chased us."

John motioned for Ambrose to hand him the hat. He looked at the name again. "He was snooping around at the gunpowder factory. Maybe he even knew about the shipment of gunpowder."

"He's the key to all of this." Ambrose nodded and took the hat back. "We just have to find out who was telling him everything."

"There *are* spies in our area," said Berty as he helped John to his feet.

"And how do you catch a spy?" Ambrose asked.

John shook his head. "Oh, no you don't, brother!"

Ambrose sucked in a deep breath as if feeling new life. "You become a spy." After a deep exhale, he said plainly, "Brothers, it's time for a little spying action of our own."

CHAPTER 22

THE COMMENDATION

Wethersfield, CT

July 1778

Rays of brilliant sunlight streamed into the tavern through the tall glass windows and open front door. The only thing brighter than the room was Ambrose's smile as he sat beside his brother John. Ambrose clanked his pewter mug against John's and took a drink of cold spring water. He winked at his father who sat across from them next to Major Benjamin Tallmadge. A barmaid in a blue dress with a white scarf around her head strolled by carrying a plate of roasted turkey to the table next to them. Ambrose's mouth watered at the smell.

"That was pretty clever," Ambrose said to the major, tearing his eyes from the turkey. "You told David Bushnell you had delayed your plans to attack the fort."

"I had to do something to deter you," Tallmadge replied. "But it seems nothing can stop you." He shook his head.

John put both hands on the table, palms down. "Only because our brother was involved," he said.

"You're lucky I didn't shoot you on the spot when I saw you at the fort." Tallmadge looked at the boys sternly. "The thought did cross my mind."

Ambrose couldn't tell if the major was joking, but John smiled. "The anger you felt seeing us only made you more fierce toward the enemy," John said.

Come on, major, crack a smile.

Tallmadge's eyes twinkled for a second. He coughed into his hand and changed the subject. "My intelligence operators inform me that you boys are asking questions at the former gunpowder factory and are now doing a little spying of your own." Major Tallmadge took a drink from his cup. By his tone, he wasn't pleased.

"Um . . . yes, sir," Ambrose admitted.

John gulped. "With some help from our father and Berty." He glanced across the table at Lamberton.

"I know." The major nodded. "Your father is my source of intelligence about this." He paused. "Spying— untrained—is a dangerous and life-threatening business," he said seriously. "If one is to be involved in such a venture one should be well-trained. We'll talk about that later. But first . . ." The major reached into his jacket and pulled out a piece of paper. "I want to read something I think you'll find of interest, from our Continental Congress." Major

Tallmadge cleared his throat. He gave the boys a small smile, unfolded the paper, and tilted his head. He began to read out loud:

In Congress

The United States Congress assembled, having taken into consideration the report of General George Washington, respecting the conduct of Ambrose and John Clark, do resolve that the thanks of the United States in Congress assembled be given to the Clark youth, for the zeal, bravery, and perseverance with which they have supported the honor of the American flag; for their bold and successful enterprises to transport valuable gunpowder helping protect the province of Connecticut; for sinking an enemy ship; for redeeming from captivity patriot soldiers who had fallen under the power of the enemy; and in general for the good conduct and eminent services by which they have added luster to their character and to the American arms.

By order of the Congress, June 1778
John Jay, President

"My, my," Lamberton Clark said gruffly. "Quite an honor."

"Indeed," Major Tallmadge replied. "And well-deserved. Congratulations, gentlemen."

In awe, Ambrose reached for the letter. But Tallmadge pulled the candle on the table closer to him and gently placed the corner of the letter over the flame. The parchment caught the flame and it quickly burned.

John's eyes widened. "Wait! Why'd you—"

"We must *not* have any evidence of your operation . . . for your own safety." The major kept close watch on the flame as it drew closer to his fingers. "But you should know the congressional librarian has crafted a copy and, should we win this war, it will be on record for generations to come."

Ambrose peered over the major's shoulder. A stranger, wearing an overcoat, got up from a barstool and walked across the room.

It's awfully warm to be wearing a coat like that, Ambrose thought to himself.

The man did not seem to be drunk, but he bumped into another man and something, some item, passed between them. The man who had been bumped quickly exited the tavern.

Ambrose memorized their faces. He turned to John who had also watched the whole scene. For certain, a message had been passed between those men. They must be spies. But for whom? Probably not for America, or Tallmadge would have known about them. No, they were most likely Tory Loyalists.

Ambrose hesitated and glanced at John again. Should they do something? There was only one way to find out whose side the men were on. They had to move fast.

John jerked a nod.

There was no time for training, no matter what Major Tallmadge said. They needed to follow these men—immediately.

"Father . . . Major . . ." Ambrose stood up.

John rose to his feet as well. "Please excuse us."

Ambrose looked at his twin. "We . . . ah . . ." Ambrose glanced out the window. The man rushed across the street.

John scratched his head. "We need to—"

"Go to the outhouse." Ambrose finished his brother's sentence and darted for the door. His eyes searched the street for either of the two men. Seconds later, John was by his side.

"Great, now the major thinks twins even go to the outhouse together," John said.

"I do have to go," admitted Ambrose.

John laughed. "Me too."

"There they are," Ambrose said, as he glanced to the left and right. They were walking in opposite directions. "But first . . . we have to follow those two."

THE END

ACKNOWLEDGMENTS

My father and I would like to thank the talented and creative editors who helped make our story so much better. To Mary Hassinger, Leslie Peterson, and Britta Eastburg from HarperCollins Christian Publishing/ Zondervan, we say a big thank you! You are the best and we appreciate the care, imagination, and expertise behind all you do. Additionally, this book series would not have happened were it not for Kim Childress, formerly of Zondervan, who served as our biggest fan and champion. Thank you, all, for loving our story and characters—and for giving your hearts to this project. You are all true patriots!

NOTES FROM THE STORYTELLERS

Although mentioned in our story, Benjamin Franklin did not provide any design improvement ideas to Mr. Bushnell for the *Turtle* submarine.

The Glastonbury Gunpowder Factory was actually destroyed by an explosion on August 23, 1777, apparently caused by lightning or static from fine powder being made that day. We had the factory still being in existence to aid the telling of our story.

Additionally, we loved the name of the British ship—the *HMS Lively*, knowing the *Turtle* in our story would render its name useless. The real *HMS Lively* was launched by the British in 1756, captured by the French in 1778, recaptured in 1781, and eventually sold in 1784.

The existence of the *Turtle* was supposed to be a secret. However, the British did know about the *Turtle* thanks to a Loyalist postmaster who read letters from one of Bushnell's friends who knew and had written about the invention. British military leaders saw it as a potential threat. The *Turtle* did have several missions but each one failed to accomplish its goal to blow up a ship.

The battle of Fort St. George took place on November

23, 1780. Only one of Tallmadge's men was wounded. The Dragoons killed seven, and captured 54. Numerous non-combatants were also captured.

In our story, General Washington's advice to the twins: "Labor to keep alive in your breast that little spark of celestial fire called conscience" was Rule Number 110 of *Washington's Rules of Civility and Decent Behavior*. The complete listing of George Washington's mandates for successful interactions with others and how to best conduct one's self is interesting and full of advice that still works today.

Oath of Allegiance

When people take a cause very seriously, and want others to know about their commitment to what they believe in, they often make a public promise called an oath. Very often, an oath is said aloud in front of others, such as a swearing in of new citizens to our country, joining a military service, when a person is promising to tell the truth in a court of law, or when a person is entering public office, like the president of the United States. Each oath is different but the reason for an oath of any kind is the same—to let others know you are serious and sure about a decision and a commitment you are making.

Colonial patriots took an oath of allegiance to the newly forming country that would be independent of Great Britian and King George.

If you were a patriot, like Ambrose, John, Lamberton, and Berty you would have probably taken an oath similar to the one below.

Place your name in the blank in the oath below and commit your allegiance to the United States of America and liberty. Add a role like courier, soldier, fife and drummer, or spy in the space provided as well.

OATH OF ALLEGIANCE

I, _____, do acknowledge the United States of America, to be Free, Independent and Sovereign States, and declare that the people thereof owe no allegiance or obedience to George the Third, King of Great-Britain, and I renounce, refute and abjure any allegiance or obedience to him; and I will, to the utmost of my power, support, maintain and defend the said United States, against the said King George the Third, his heirs and successors and his or their abettors, affiliants and adherents, and will serve the said United States in the office of _____, which I now hold, with fidelity, according to the best of my skill and understanding.

DISCUSSION QUESTIONS

1. Why did the colonists call themselves patriots?

2. If you were Ambrose, would you have volunteered to pilot the *Turtle*? Why or why not?

3. What role did fear of dying play in Ambrose's life? What are some things that might make you feel real fear? What helps you overcome fear?

4. Why did Bushnell invent the original *Turtle*?

5. Why was the *Turtle* impressive for its time?

6. Have you ever invented something? Where did the idea come from? If you actually developed the invention, how did it make you feel to have a finished product?

7. Ambrose had a talent for sailing (among many other things). John was an expert marksman and planner. What are your talents? Where do your talents come from? How can you use them for a fulfilled life?

8. Washington said in the story and in real life, "Labor to keep alive in your breast that little spark of celestial fire called conscience." What do you think he meant by that? Explain your thinking.

9. When Ambrose thought twice about going into battle at the fort, John encouraged him and reminded his brother that he "had his back." Have you ever been in a situation when you reconsidered something you felt committed to or had to encourage someone else to take a risk? Describe the situation.

10. What issues are worth fighting, arguing, or dying for, in your opinion?

11. How is freedom not free?

12. Define bravery. When did Ambrose display bravery? When did John show he was brave? When have you displayed bravery in your life?

13. In the story, Berty endured great physical pain and still didn't give the enemy any secrets in order to save his brothers and the colonists' gunpowder. Would you be willing to suffer for something to that level?

14. Parents and leaders need to often make difficult decisions. Lamberton Clark, the boys' father, wondered if he had risked too much by putting his family in harm's way. Why must leaders sometimes do such things? Do you think it's easy? How have you benefitted from the sacrifices of others?

15. Although Ambrose and John are twins, they have very different personalities. Describe how they are similar and how they are different and explain why you think this.

16. Sergeant Evans was considered an enemy in the story. As part of the British army, he fought against the patriots and probably hurt or killed many men. In your opinion, was he just as brave as the Clarks? Does standing up for a cause you believe in, no matter what the cause, make you brave?

17. At the end of the story, the twins received a commendation from the Continental Congress. Why is it important to recognize the efforts people make? What have you been recognized for? How did the recognition make you feel?

18. Do you think your own life has been impacted by the outcome of the American Revolution? If yes, give three examples.

19. Throughout the story, many of the characters pray for courage for themselves and for others. What do you pray for? How do you pray?

20. Is it being disobedient for Ambrose and John to take matters into their own hands, putting themselves in danger?

HISTORICAL CHARACTERS

DAVID BUSHNELL
(1740–1824)

David Bushnell was an American inventor and veteran of the Revolutionary War. While studying at Yale College in 1775, Bushnell created the first submarine ever used in combat. His idea to use water as ballast for submerging and raising his submarine, called the *Turtle*, is still in use today. While a student at Yale, Bushnell proved gunpowder could be exploded under water. He also invented the first time bomb. The *Turtle* combined these ideas to attack ships by attaching a time bomb to their hulls, while using a hand-powered drill and ship auger bit to penetrate the hulls.

Bushnell used the *Turtle* in attempts to attack British ships blockading New York Harbor in the summer of 1776. Unfortunately, his efforts failed every time because the *Turtle's* boring device could not penetrate the copper sheeting lining the British ships' hulls, which was designed to protect them against parasites. The first *Turtle* sank while retreating from British observation, but a Bushnell family member who was serving as the sole commander was able to bail out and survive.

In 1781, Bushnell was commissioned as a captain in the Continental Army. He fought in the Siege of Yorktown the following September and October, the only time the unit had the opportunity to serve in combat. After the Revolutionary War, General George Washington presented a medal to David Bushnell. He died in Georgia in 1824.

CALEB GIBBS
(1748—1818)

Caleb Gibbs was a captain in the Fourteenth Massachusetts Regiment. In 1776, General Washington picked Gibbs to command his newly established personal guard, officially known as the "Commander-in-Chief's Guard," and unofficially called the "Life Guards." It was a unique position. Gibbs was considered a member of General Washington's family, but he was also an army officer with combat command. In addition to protecting the Commander-in-Chief and the headquarters, Gibbs was responsible for selecting defensible quarters for General Washington and his staff when the army was on the move. When the General was traveling, Major Gibbs often mounted a guard to accompany him.

NATHAN HALE
(June 6, 1755—September 22, 1776)

Hale was a young but passionate soldier for the Continental Army. When he was twenty-one, Hale volunteered for an intelligence-gathering mission in New York City, but the British captured him. He is best remembered for his last words said before being hanged: "I only regret that I have but one life to give for my country."

GOLD SILLIMAN
(1732–1790)

A native of Fairfield, Connecticut, Gold Silliman graduated from Yale University and practiced law as a crown attorney before the Revolution. During the War for Independence, Silliman became a militia general. In May 1775, he was appointed as a colonel of the Fourth Regiment Connecticut Militia and became brigadier general in 1776. In 1779, Silliman and his son were captured in their home by Tories and held prisoner until an exchange could be arranged a year later.

BENJAMIN TALLMADGE
(1754–1835)

Benjamin Tallmadge was the son of a church leader. He graduated from Yale College in 1773, where he was a class-mate of American Revolutionary War spy Nathan Hale. Tallmadge was a major in the Second Continental Light Dragoons, but eventually he was promoted to the rank of colonel and became the chief intelligence officer for George Washington. In this position, he organized the Culper Spy Ring based out of New York City and Long Island.

GLOSSARY

American Turtle The *American Turtle* was the world's first submersible used in combat. David Bushnell built it in Old Saybrook, Connecticut, in 1775 as a means of attaching explosive charges to British Royal Navy vessels occupying North American harbors during the Revolutionary War. Connecticut Governor Jonathan Trumbull recommended the invention to George Washington. The commander-in-chief was skeptical, but he provided funds and support for the development and testing of the vessel.

In 1776, the *Turtle* made several attempts to attach explosives to the hulls of British warships in New York Harbor. All failed. The *Turtle's* transport ship was sunk later that year by the British with the submarine aboard. Bushnell said he recovered the machine, but its final fate is unknown.

The Battle of Fort St. George The Battle of Fort St. George was a raid on a fortified Loyalist outpost and storage depot on Long Island led by Major Benjamin Tallmadge on November 23, 1780. Tallmadge's raid was a success—the garrison was surprised, and provisions and prisoners were captured.

Many Loyalist refugees from Rhode Island lived at Fort St. George where they fortified the property, erecting a stockade twelve feet high in a triangular shape around the manor house. The stockade was lined with sharpened tree branches and a deep ditch.

Major Tallmadge led a force of about eighty men from his 2nd Continental Light Dragoons and ordered his men to leave their muskets unloaded and bayonets fixed. He divided his force into three, with each unit to attack one of the stockade's sides. Tallmadge's party was not spotted until it was within forty yards of the stockade. A sentry fired his weapon to raise the alarm, but there wasn't time for the Tories to organize a proper defense. The group, led by Tallmadge, rushed the stockade and cut its way through, while two other units scaled the wall, and the main house was surrounded and surrendered in less than ten minutes. Some of the Loyalist garrison reached a fortified house that formed part of the stockade, but they surrendered after a brief firefight.

Bayonet A blade attached to the muzzle of a rifle and used for hand-to-hand combat

Continental Congress A meeting of representatives from the thirteen colonies during the American Revolutionary War that eventually became the governing body of the newly formed United States of America. This group met between 1774 and 1789.

Culper Spy Ring British forces occupied New York in August 1776, and the city remained a British stronghold and a major naval base for the rest of the Revolutionary War. Though getting information from New York about British troop movements and other plans was critical to General George Washington, there was simply no reliable intelligence network that existed on the Patriot side. But that changed in 1778 when a young cavalry officer named Benjamin Tallmadge established a small group of trustworthy men and women from his hometown of Setauket, Long Island. Known as the Culper Spy Ring, named after the aliases of its main members, Samuel Culper, Sr. and Samuel Culper, Jr., Tallmadge's network became the most effective of any intelligence-gathering operation on either side during the Revolutionary War.

Frigate During the Revolutionary War period, this was a warship built for speed and maneuverability. A frigate usually had guns mounted on deck and three masts.

Lobsterback A slang term used by Americans for British soldiers because the red coats worn by the British resembled the red shells of cooked lobsters.

Loyalists American colonists who remained loyal to Great Britain during the American Revolutionary War. They were also called Tories, Royalists, or King's Men. They were opposed by the Patriots, those who supported the Revolution. When their cause was defeated, about twenty percent of the Loyalists fled to other parts of the British Empire, many to Ontario and New Brunswick, Canada. It has been estimated that between fifteen and twenty percent of the European-American population of the colonies were Loyalists.

Musket A muzzle-loaded, smooth bore long gun, fired from the shoulder. Muskets were designed for use by infantry and included a bayonet.

North River The North River was also referred to as the Hudson River on some maps in the eighteenth century. It is commonly called the Hudson River today.

The Sons of Liberty A political group made up of American patriots that originated in the pre-independence colonies. The group was formed to protect the rights of the colonists from the British government after 1766. They are best known for the Boston Tea Party in 1773, which led to the Intolerable Acts (an intense crackdown by the British government). The Patriots' counter-mobilization to these Acts led directly to the American Revolutionary War in 1775.

Tory See **Loyalists**

West Point West Point, in the state of New York, was a fortified site during the Revolutionary War. Founded by one of the best military men of the time, Polish General Tadeusz Kościuszko, the site was strategically chosen for the abnormal S-curve in the nearby Hudson River. West Point was manned by a small garrison of Continental soldiers through the entirety of the war. A great iron chain was stretched across the Hudson at this point in order to impede British Navy vessels, but its usefulness was never tested. The site consisted of multiple fortifications, including Fort Putnam, which is still preserved in a Revolutionary-period design.

Historical Letters

Author Note: The following letters reflect the spelling and punctuation of the time, which may be different from what we find correct today.

LETTER FROM GEORGE WASHINGTON TO THOMAS JEFFERSON
Mount Vernon 26th Sept. 1785

I am sorry I cannot give you full information respecting Captn. Bushnals projects for the destruction of shipping. No interesting experiment having been made, and my memory being treacherous, I may, in some measure, be mistaken in what I am about to relate.

Bushnel is a man of great Mechanical powers—fertile of invention—and a master in execution—He came to me in 1776 recommended by Governor Trumbull (now dead) and other respectable characters who were proselites to his plan.—Although I wanted faith myself, I furnished him with money, and other aids to carry it into execution.—He laboured for some time ineffectually, & though the advocates for his scheme continued sanguine he never did succeed—One accident or another was always intervening.—I then thought, and still think, that it was an effort of genius; but that a combination of too many things were requisite, to expect much success from the enterprise against an enemy, who are always upon guard.

That he had a machine which was so contrived as to carry a man under water at any depth he chose, and for a considerable time & distance, with an apparatus charged with Powder which he could fasten to a ship's bottom or side & give fire to in any given time (sufft. for him to retire) by means whereof a ship could be blown up, or sunk, are facts which I believe admit of little doubt—but then, where it was to operate against an enemy, it is no easy matter to get a person hardy enough to encounter the variety of dangers to which he must be exposed. 1 from the novelty 2 from the difficulty of conducting the machine, and governing it under water on acct. of the Currents &ca. 3 the consequent uncertainty of hitting the object of destination, without rising frequently above water for fresh observation, wch., when near the Vessel, would expose the adventurer to a discovery, & almost to certain death.

To these causes I always ascribed the non-performance of his plan, as he wanted nothing that I could furnish to secure the success of it.—This to the best of my recollection is a true state of the case—But Humphreys, if I mistake not, being one of the proselites, will be able to give you a more perfect acct. of it than I have done.

Source: Papers of Thomas Jefferson, vol. 13, Library of Congress, Washington, DC. Printed in Thomas Jefferson,

The Papers of Thomas Jefferson, ed. by Julian Boyd, et al., 34 vols. to date. Princeton: Princeton University Press, 1950-, 8: 555–57.

For more information about the American *Turtle*, visit http://www.history.navy.mil/library/online/sub_turtle.htm#item12

LETTER FROM EZRA LEE (FIRST CAPTAIN OF THE TURTLE) TO DAVID HUMPHREYS
Lyme 20th Feb. 1815.

Dr. Sir,

Judge Griswold, & Charles Griswold Esq. both informed me that you wished to have an account of a machine invented by David Bushnell of Saybrook, at the commencement of our Revolutionary war. In the summer of 1776, he went to New York with it to try the *Asia* man of war:—his brother being acquainted with the working of the machine, was to try the first experiment with it, but having spent until the middle of August, he gave out, in consequence of indisposition.—Mr. Bushnell then came to General Parsons (of Lyme) to get someone to go, and learn the ways & mystery of this new machine, and to make a trial of it.

General Parsons, sent for me, & two others, who had given in our names to go in a fire ship if wanted, to see if we would undertake the enterprize:—we agreed to it, but first returned with the machine down Sound, and on our way practised with it in several harbours.—we returned as far back as Say-Brook with Mr Bushnell, where some little alterations were made in it—in the course of which time, (it being 8 or 10 days) the British had got possession of Long Island & Governor's Island—We went back as far as New Rochelle and had it carted over by land to the North River.—

Before I proceed further, I will endeavour to give you some idea of the construction of this machine, *turtle* or torpedo, as it has since been called.—(1) Its shape was most like a round clam, but longer, and set up on its square side—it was high enough to stand in or sit as you had occasion, with a (2) composition head hanging on hinges.— it had six glasses, inserted in the head, and made water tight, each the size of a half Dollar piece, to admit light— in a clear day, a person might see to read in three fathoms of water—The machine was steered by a rudder having a crooked tiller, which led in by your side, through a water joint.—(3) then sitting on the seat, the navigator rows with one hand, & steers with the other—it had two oars, of about 12 inches in length, & 4 or 5 in width, shaped like the arms of a windmill, which led also inside through water joints, in front of the person steering, and were worked by means of a wench (or crank) and with hard labour, the machine might be impelled at the rate of 3 knots an hour for a short time—Seven hundred pounds of lead were fixed on the bottom for ballast, and two hundred weight of it was so contrived, as to let it go in case the pumps choaked, so that you could rise at the surface of the water.—It was sunk by letting in water by a spring near the bottom, by placing your foot against which, the water would rush in and when sinking take off your foot & it would cease to come in & you would sink no further, but if you had sunk too far, pump out water until you got the necessary depth—these pumps forced the water out at the bottom, one being on each side of you as you rowed—A pocket compass was fixed in the side, with a piece of light (4) wood on the north side, thus +, and another on the east side thus, to steer by while under water—Three round doors were cut in the head, (each 3 inches diameter) to let in fresh air, untill you wished to sink, and then they were shut down & fastened—There was also a glass tube (5) 12 inches long and 1 inch diamater, with a cork in it, with a peice of light wood, fixed to it, and another peice at the bottom of the tube, to tell the depth of discent,—one inch rise of the cork in the tube gave about one fathom water,—It had a screw, that peirced through the top of the machine, with a water joint, which was so very sharp that it would enter wood, with very little force, and this was turned with a wench, or crank, and when entered fast in the bottom of the ship, the screw is then left, and the machine is disengaged, by unscrewing another one inside that held the other.

From the screw now fixed on the bottom of the ship, a line—led to & fastened to the magazine, to prevent its escape either side of the ship—the magazine was directly behind you on the outside, and that was faced from you by unscrewing a screw inside—Inside the magazine was a clock machinery, which immediately sets a going after it is disengaged & a gun lock is fixed to strike fire to the powder, at the set time after the Clock should rundown—The clock might be set to go longer or shorter—20 or 30 minutes was the usual time, to let the navigator escape—This magazine was shaped like an egg, & made of oak dug out in two peices, bound together with bands of iron, corked & paid over with tar so as to be perfectly tight, and the clock was bound so as not to run untill this magazine was unscrewed. . . . .

I will now endeavour to give you a short account of my voyage in this machine.—The first night after we got down to New York with it, that was favourable, (for the time for a trial, must be, when it is slack water, & calm, as it is unmanagable in a swell or a strong tide) the British Fleet lay a little above Staten Island We set off from the City—the Whale boats towed me as nigh the ships, as they dared to go, and then cast me off—I soon found that it was too early in the tide, as it carried me down by the ships—I however hove about, and rowed for 5 glasses, by the ships' bells, before the tide slacked so that I, could get along side of the man of war, which lay above the transports—

The Moon was about 2 hours high, and the daylight about one—when I rowed under the stern of the ship, could see the men on deck, & hear them talk—I then shut down all the doors, sunk down, and came under the bottom of the ship, up with the screw against the bottom but found that it would not enter—(6) I pulled along to try another place, but deviated a little one side, and immediately rode with great velocity, and come above the surface 2 or 3 feet between the ship and the daylight—then sunk again like a porpoise I hove partly about to try again, but on further thought I gave out, knowing that as soon as it was light the ships boats would be rowing in all directions, and I thought the best generalship, was to retreat, as fast as I could as I had 4 miles to go, before passing Governor's Island.—

So I jogg'd on as fast as I could, and my compass being then of no use to me, I was obliged to rise up every few minutes to see that I sailed in the right direction, and for this purpose keeping the machine on the surface of the water, and the doors open—I was much afraid of getting aground on the island as the Tide of the flood set on the north point While on my passage up to the City, my course owing to the above circumstances, was very crooked & zig zag, and the enemy's attention was drawn towards me, from Governors Island—

When I was abreast of the fort on the island 3 or 400 men got upon the parapet to observe me,—at leangth a number came down to the shore, shoved off a 12 oar'd barge, with 5 or 6 sitters, and pulled for me—I eyed them, and when they had got within 50 or 60 yards of me, I let loose the magazine, in hopes, that if they should take me, they would likewise pick up the magazine, and then we should all be blown up together, but as kind Providence would have it, they took fright, and returned to the island, to my infinite joy.—I then weathered the Island, and our people seeing me, came off with a whaleboat, and towed me in—The Magazine after getting a little past the Island, went off with a tremendous explosion, throwing up large bodies of water to an immense height. (7)

Before we had another opportunity to try an experiment our army evacuated New York, and we retreated up the North River as far as fort Lee—A Frigate came up and anchored off Bloomingdale. I now made another attempt upon a new plan—my intention was to have gone under the ship's stern, and screwed on the magazine close to the water's edge, but I was discovered by the Watch and was obliged to abondon this scheme, then shutting my doors, I dove under her, but my cork in the tube, (by which I ascertained my depth) got obstructed, and deceived me, and I descended too deep & did not track the ship, and I then left her—Soon after the Frigate came up the river, drove our Crane galley on shore, and sunk our Sloop, from which we escaped to the shore—

I am &c. E. Lee.

For General David Humphreys-

(1) This machine was built of oak, in the strongest manner possible, corked and tarred, and though its sides were at least six inches thick, the writer of the forgoing, told me that the pressure of the water, against it, at the depth of two fathoms was so great, that it oozed quite through, as mercury will by means of the air pump. Mr. Bushnell's machine was no larger than just to admit one person to navigate:— its extreme leangth was not more than 7. feet.—When lying in the water, in its ordinary state without ballasts, its upper

works did not rise more than 6 or 7 inches out of water—

(2) This composition head, means of composition of Metals—something like bell metal, and was fixed on the top of the machine, and which afforded the only admission to the inside—

(3) The steering of this machine was done on the same principles, with ordinary vessels, but the rowing her through the water, was on a very different plan—These oars, were fixed on the end of a shaft like windmill arms, projected out, forward, and turned at right angles with the course of the machine, and upon the same principles that windmill arms are turned, by the wind these oars, when put in motion as the writer describes, draws the machine slowly after it—this moving power is small, and every attendant circumstance, must cooperate with it, to answer the purpose, calm waters & no current—

(4) This light wood is what we *sometimes* call fox fire, and is the dry wood that shines in the dark:—this was necessary as the points of the compass could not readily be seen without—

(5) The glass tube here mentioned, which was a sort of thermometer, to ascertain the depth of water the machine descended, is the only part that is without explanation—the writer of the forgoing, could not reccollect the principles on which such an effect, was produced, nor the mechanical contrivance of it—He only knows that it was so contrived that the cork & light wood rose or fell in the tubes, by the ascent or descent of the machine—

(6) The reason why the screw would not enter, was that the ship's bottom being coppered it would have been difficult under any circumstances to have peirced through it—but on attempting to bore with the auger, the force necessary to be used in pressing against the ships bottom, caused the machine to rebound off this difficulty defeated the whole.—the screw could not enter the bottom, and of course the magazine could not be kept there in the mode desired—

(7) When the explosion took place, General Putnam was vastly pleased, and cried out in his piculiar way—"God's curse 'em, that'll do it for 'em."[1]

Source: Yale University Library. A slightly modified version of the letter was published in *The Magazine of American History*, vol. 29 (January-June 1893).

---

1 These explanatory notes were apparently added by Humphreys.

Patriots, Redcoats and Spies

Rob J. Skead with Robert A. Skead

When Revolutionary War Patriot Lamberton Clark is shot by British soldiers while on a mission for the Continental Army, he has only two hopes of getting the secret message he's carrying to General George Washington: his 14-year-old twin boys John and Ambrose. They set off from Connecticut to New Jersey to find General Washington, but the road to the commander-in-chief of the Continental Army is full of obstacles; including the man who shot their father who is hot on their trail.

Available in stores and online!